Lore of the Reef Lights
Life in the Florida Keys

Thomas W. Taylor

ISBN 978-0-7414-3471-5

Front Cover Photo of Thomas W. Taylor by Judith S. Trotter.

Front Cover Design by Renee Anderson.

Back Cover Photo by Paul DeMoranville.

Published by:
INFINITY
PUBLISHING.COM
1094 New DeHaven Street, Suite 100
West Conshohocken, PA 19428-2713
Info@buybooksontheweb.com
www.buybooksontheweb.com
Toll-free (877) BUY BOOK
Local Phone (610) 941-9999
Fax (610) 941-9959

Printed in the United States of America

Published December 2006

Editors:
Neil E. Hurley
Gail Swanson

Technical Assistance:
Dan Gallagher

Financial Assistance Providers:
Jim Boyle
George Evans
Dan Gallagher
Richard A. Johnson
Eric Martin
John Parkhust
Harry & Jean Pettit
Betty Lowe Phelps
Ben & Barbara Revell
Historical Preservation Society of the Upper Keys, Inc.,
Jerry Wilkinson, President
Thomas W. Taylor Memorial Fund of
The Florida Keys Reef Lights Foundation, Inc.,
Richard Schulze, President
Contributors to the Fund:
Toni (Lowe) & Bryon Clinger
Grace H. Dodge
George & Nancy Hutchinson
Eric Martin
Christopher & Elizabeth Phelps
The Marathon Sailing Club

Table of Contents

Editor's Preface

by Gail Swanson

Wayne Wheeler, President of the United States Lighthouse Society, wrote of lighthouse historian and author Thomas W. Taylor that he was: "one of our nation's premier experts on the subject." Tom Taylor was an extraordinary man and a prolific writer, with five other books on lighthouses to his credit.

While preparing my friend Tom Taylor's book, *The Key West Lighthouse, A Light in Paradise*, for publication after his death I learned that Tom had been planning a book after that one. He wrote in it, "This is the second book in Mr. Taylor's 'Florida Lighthouse Series'....To be published in 2005 will be his third book... *Lore of the Reef Lights: Life in the Florida Keys.*"

With the permission of Tom's mother Jeanne Taylor I had temporary possession of all of Tom's paper files, and by the keen attention of Marathon resident and fellow historian Dan Gallagher all of Tom's computer files had been copied. There was no finding anything in the disorganized mass of papers, so I checked his computer files. There, indeed, were articles Tom had written on the keepers of the Florida Reef lights, some of which had been printed in the Marathon-Big Pine Key *Free Press* and others that hadn't been. It was these articles, with others of Tom's on the little-known lightships stationed at the reef and on the lighthouses built on the reef that, put together, is the work you hold in your hands. I believe that this is close to what Tom planned for his Lore book. All the writing, except in the appendix, is Tom's, although some of the articles were shortened or rearranged for flow for book form.

Lighthouse expert Neil E. Hurley became, thankfully, my co-editor. Without Dan and Neil and other friends of Tom's who financially contributed to the cost of publication this book would not have been possible.

Thomas W. Taylor was born March 12, 1949 in Columbus, Ohio, first child of four of Thomas William "Bill" Taylor and Jeanne Blank Taylor. He earned a bachelor's degree cum laude in international studies from Ohio State University in 1971 and another bachelor's from the same school in 1976 in education. That year he became involved in American Bicentennial historical re-enactments and won the Special Merit Award for Research and Program Presentation from the Early American Society. For over nine years he worked at several historic sites for the National Park Service, including two Florida sites, and earned a master's degree in public history and museum administration from the University of North Carolina at Greensboro in 1984, after which he returned to Florida. He was, for seven years, the historian at the Ponce de Leon Inlet Lighthouse. In 1994 he won the Keeper of the Quarter Award from the United States Lighthouse Society. He was a consultant and actor in three motion pictures, IMAX's "Alamo: The Price of Freedom," "Glory," and "The Rose and the Jackal." More on his achievements is in his beloved sister Kay's eulogy I placed at the end of this book.

In 2001 Tom moved to Marathon, Middle Florida Keys, to sail, SCUBA dive, work toward preserving the offshore reef lights and, he told me, to concentrate on writing. He passed away May 19, 2004, at his home in Marathon from heart failure.

Part 1
Lightships of the Florida Keys

Introduction

Soon after Florida became a territory of the United States in 1821, commercial interests in Louisiana and New York began pressuring Congress for navigational aids in Florida. Ever since the Louisiana Purchase in 1803, much of the commerce between the central part of the new nation and the eastern ports had come down the Mississippi River, through New Orleans, and then through the Straits of Florida between Florida and Cuba, and then up the Atlantic coast. The most dangerous part of this voyage was the narrow Florida Straits, bordered by the treacherous coral reefs of the Florida Keys from the Dry Tortugas to Cape Florida on Key Biscayne.

Through the persistence of Louisiana Congressman, Josiah Johnston, on May 7, 1822, Congress authorized the construction of lighthouses at Cape Florida and in the Dry Tortugas, but everyone knew that this was just the beginning of lighting the dangerous Florida Keys and that other lights were desperately needed in between. In April, 1824, James Ramage submitted a report to the Secretary of the Navy, wherein he informed the Secretary about "the extensive Reef of Carysfort which here commences and extends to a great distance from the shore." Carysfort Reef, which had been named for a British frigate grounded there in 1770, extended out so far, that Ramage felt that "the erection of a

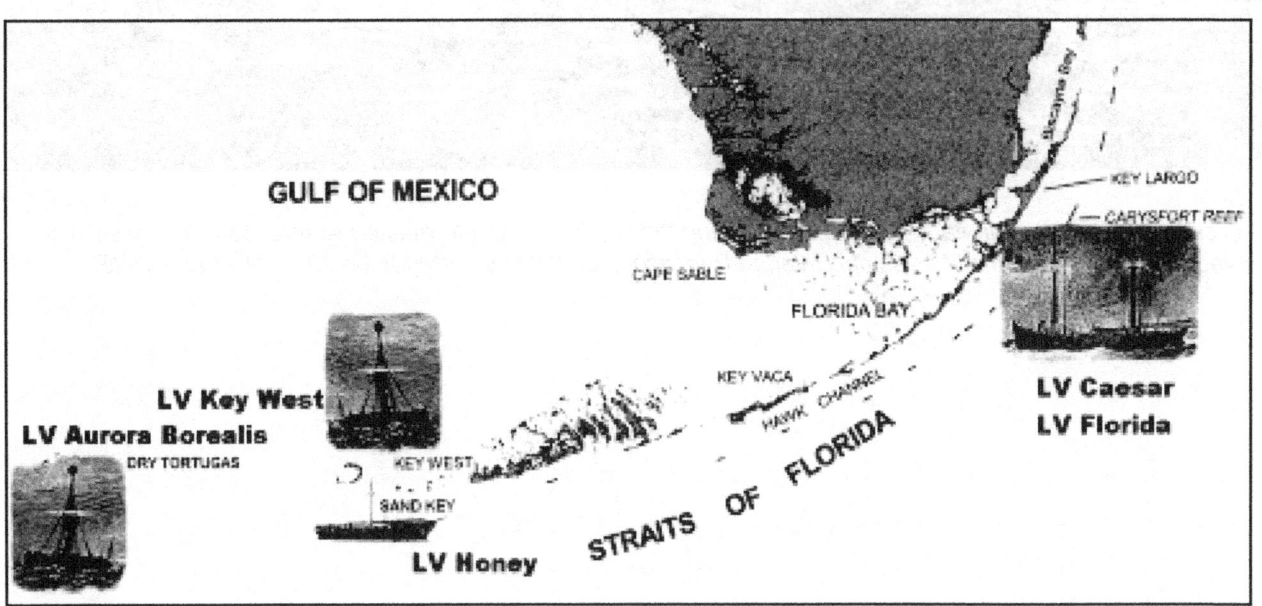

Map of the Florida Keys showing the locations of the lightships that were the first signals along the reefline.

Ed Note: The materials in this section from pages 5 through 18 were printed in The Keepers Log, *Vol. 21, No. 1 (October-December 2004), and are reprinted here by permission of the United States Lighthouse Society.*

Beacon on the shore [is] but of little use." He suggested that a lighthouse be constructed directly on the reef or that a light vessel be stationed there.

For a number of places in the Florida Keys, lightships were initially believed to be more cost-effective than lighthouses. There would be four lightship stations established, and five vessels would serve on the reefs in the Florida Keys. They would protect mariners until the technology for building iron-pile lighthouses was developed to permit the lightships to be replaced by this unique and special type of lighthouse.

This sketch is typical of an early lightship resembling the tiny 50-ton single-masted Aurora Borealis *vessel which served off the mouth of the Mississippi River, at Pensacola, and at Dry Tortugas between 1821 and 1825.*

The Dry Tortugas Lightship (1825-1826):
Aurora Borealis

In 1825-1826, while the early Dry Tortugas Lighthouse on Garden Key was under construction, it was deemed necessary to mark the dangerous shoals of that area. A light vessel was stationed there. The only documentation found so far for this vessel, which also indicates that it had more than just lights aboard, is found in an account in the *East Florida Herald* of St. Augustine for June 6, 1826. In this issue, Captain Josiah Doane of the United States Revenue Cutter *Marion* at Key West, reported that he was "gratified to learn that the Light vessel on the Dry Tortugas has been of the most essential service in warning vessels of approaching danger. Four ships lately have been entirely indebted to the warnings of the bells of the light vessel." Although government documents positively identifying this vessel have not yet been located, it is almost certain that this vessel was the *Aurora Borealis*, one of the first lightships built in the United States.

In January, 1818, the United States government signed a contract with Winslow Lewis for building the first lighthouse at the mouth of the Mississippi River, on Frank's Island, Louisiana. Lewis' first attempt did not succeed due to the soft, silty bottom which swallowed the foundation. The structure was scheduled to be completed by April 1st, 1820, but by the end of January, it was apparent that the lighthouse would never be ready in time for the busy summer shipping season. Stephen Pleasonton, in charge of America's lighthouses, persuaded Congress to authorize the construction of a "vessel to serve as a floating light," to be moored off the mouth of the Mississippi until such time as the new lighthouse could finally be completed. Pleasonton succeeded in getting his authorization, but it was not until August 10, 1820, that a contract was signed with Christian Bergh to build the new lightship for $7,925.58. Measuring probably less than 60 feet long, the new fifty-ton vessel would have two masts, between which the lantern was suspended. Launched and christened *Aurora Borealis* that winter, she took up her station soon afterwards. For more than two years, while the Frank's Island lighthouse was being reconstructed, the sturdy little vessel remained at anchor off the mouth of the Mississippi, her lights beaming out at night to guide mariners safely in or safely past. When Lewis finally completed the Frank's Island Lighthouse in 1823, the *Aurora Borealis* was no longer needed. Almost immediately, Pleasonton had a new duty station in mind. On April 30, 1823, Pleasonton wrote to inform Alexander Scott, Jr., the deputy Collector of Customs at Pensacola, Florida, that Beverly Chew, "the Collector of Customs at New Orleans has been directed to send the Floating Light Vessel, which for some time has been stationed at the mouth of the Mississippi River, to Pensacola." Captain William Cranston sailed the light vessel to Pensacola, where she arrived to take up her new station on June 13, 1823. As Captain Cranston had put in for retirement, Pleasonton authorized Scott to appoint a new captain for the vessel on her arrival in Pensacola. On May 20th, John Gates was appointed as the new captain of the *Aurora Borealis*.

Life on the lightship was very tough, and the captains did not last very long. When John Gates resigned on December 1st, Collector Scott appointed John McGregor to succeed Gates. McGregor resigned after only twenty days aboard the light vessel, and on January 20, 1824, John Campbell was appointed to replace McGregor. On September 4, Captain Campbell was removed from his position for "aiding and abetting vessels to avoid the revenue laws," and Henry de Grand-Pre succeeded him.

When the new Pensacola Lighthouse was finally completed and lighted on December 20, 1824, the wave-weary *Aurora Borealis* could be removed from her forlorn anchorage and moved to another location. The new Pensacola Collector of Customs, Archibald Hamilton, requested from Stephen

Pleasonton instructions for the light vessel. Pleasonton replied that Hamilton should lay up the vessel at Pensacola until the following spring when new orders for the *Aurora Borealis* would be sent. No documents have surfaced to confirm it, but it is believed that in the spring of 1825, the first light vessel to serve in Florida waters at Pensacola moved south to fulfill the same duties at the Dry Tortugas.[1] The vessel was much needed in the Dry Tortugas as Captain Doane's report indicated that her presence had saved at least four vessels from grief on the reefs. Captain Henry de Grand-Pre would have been still in charge of the *Aurora Borealis* at the Dry Tortugas, as records show that he remained as her captain until December 21, 1826, a few months after the lighthouse had been lighted and the lightship would have been withdrawn. Where the *Aurora Borealis* went after serving at the Dry Tortugas is currently unknown.

The new lightship for the Carysfort Reef station was named Florida. She was a 220-ton vessel and served from 1831 to 1852.

The Carysfort Reef Lightships (1825-1852):
Caesar and *Florida*

In May 1824, before construction could begin on two lighthouses already authorized by Congress at Cape Florida and the Dry Tortugas, further appropriations were made for these two sites. Authorization was also given for a third lighthouse to be built on "one of the Sambo Keys" and for a "vessel for a floating light" to be stationed on the very dangerous Carysfort Reef, off the northern end of Key Largo. Twenty thousand dollars was appropriated for the building of the new light vessel.

In September 1824, the contract for the new lightship was awarded to Messrs. Isaac Webb, John Allen, and William P. Rathbone of New York. The contract was signed on the 28th. The new lightship would be a relatively large vessel of 220 tons burthen and built in frame of white oak. The contract price was for $18,500, payable when the vessel was delivered at her station.

In May, 1825, as the vessel was nearing completion, Stephen Pleasonton wrote William Pinkney, Collector of Customs for Key West, that the new light vessel would be under Pinkney's superintendence and that it would arrive at Key West in a short time. In June the year before, John Rodman, Collector of Customs for St. Augustine had proposed Captain John Whalton of that city to be the captain of the new lightship at a salary of $700 per year. At the end of May, 1825, Whalton was duly appointed by President John Quincy Adams. Whalton was directed to go to Key West to await the arrival there of his new vessel. Pinkney was to "employ a sufficient number of seamen, not exceeding six, to be stationed on board the vessel, to whom you will allow the wages usually given to seamen in the merchant service. If the hands who go with the vessel from New York are willing to remain on board, it may be well to engage them, unless you can procure others more suitable, and at a cheaper rate."

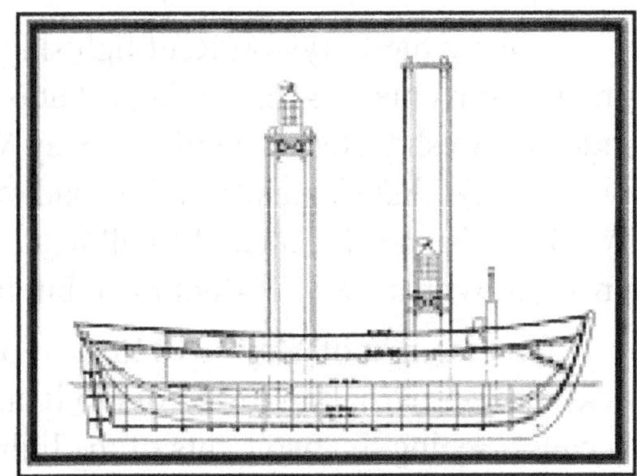

Draft plan for Carysfort Lightship.

Finally, on June 4, 1825, Jonathan Thompson, Collector of Customs for New York sent to Stephen Pleasonton the certification that the vessel had been completed. A supply of oil "sufficient to last three or four months" was put on board the vessel, and it was prepared for sea. In July, the new light vessel set sail for Key West. Her appointed captain, John Whalton, sailed from St. Augustine for Charleston, from where he would sail to Key West to rendezvous with his new charge. However, while in Charleston, on the 23rd, Whalton heard a report that the lightship had been lost on the Florida coast. Not being able to confirm the report, Whalton sailed on to Key West.

When Whalton arrived in Key West he heard the incredible news. It was hard to believe, but it was true! The loss of his new vessel was confirmed. On August 21st, F. A. Browne of Key West, hearing the report from the local wreckers, sent a letter to Pleasonton in which he said that the lightship had run ashore fifty-eight miles north of Cape Florida and had been abandoned by her captain. Pleasonton wrote to Jonathan Thompson in New York to remind Messrs Isaac Webb and Company that the ship had to be delivered "in Complete order...before payment could be made."

The wreckers salvaged the damaged hull of the lightship, refloated her, and towed her to Key West. There she fell under the gavel of the court of arbitration. The vessel was re-purchased by the contractors for $10,000. By the end of December, the vessel was being repaired, and Captain Whalton was preparing to take command of his charge. However, there were delays as a vessel coming from

Havana with lumber for the repairs was lost. It was not until mid-March, 1826, that Pinkney could certify that the lightship had been sufficiently repaired to take up her station on Carysfort Reef.

In early April, 1826, the lightship finally arrived at Carysfort Reef, six miles from Key Largo off the Basin Hill Bank. Pinkney ordered her lamps to be lighted on the 15th of that month, after a notice to that effect had had time to circulate in New York and Havana. The vessel would show "two fixed lights at 50 and 60 feet above the sea visible 4 leagues off [12 nautical miles]." Soon, Captain Whalton was calling his lightship the *Caesar*.

The lamps were lighted as proposed. At the end of the first month on station, Pinkney wrote to Pleasonton requesting awnings for the vessel and grass bagging for her sides to protect the wood of the vessel from drying and shrinking in the heat of the sun, which caused the seams to open and the vessel to leak. As the crew would have to row forty-five miles to fetch drinking water for the vessel, Pinkney decided to allow Captain Whalton one extra crew member. In mid-May, Pinkney reported the vessel's bearings as seven miles southeast of the north end of Key Largo, three to four miles north 1/2 E distance three to four miles from the elbow of Carysfort Reef. Captain Josiah Doane, of the U. S. Revenue Cutter *Marion* soon reported that he could see the lights of the light vessel from sixteen miles away.

Life on the Carysfort Reef lightship was not easy. Captain Whalton complained constantly of the great inconveniences, particularly that of obtaining provisions and water at such great distances (45 miles for fresh water, 140 miles to Key West for provisions!). Supplies for his men were so expensive in Key West that Captain Whalton had to supplement the government allowance from his own pocket. Whalton also needed a good small boat for the procurement of the supplies. He was eventually provided with a small 20-foot boat, but it proved inadequate.

On the night of May 4, 1826, a ship wrecked on Carysfort Reef very close to the lightship. The next morning Whalton rowed out to it and learned that the captain had ventured so close to the reef because, seeing the two lights of the lightship, he thought the lightship was another vessel sailing in clear water. Whalton felt sure the captain had been drunk but gathered up the gear and provisions of the wrecked vessel and housed the crew on the lightship until the wreckers could arrive.

On June 5, 1827 during one voyage to get fresh water on Key Largo, the boat was lost along with two crewmen, Hans Hansen and Thomas Van Pelt. The boat was found several days later in twelve feet of water with her sails set and no sign of the two men. They were presumed drowned.[2]

Due to the close quarters aboard the vessel and the difficult, tedious life, tensions sometimes broke out between the crew members on the light vessel. The *Savannah Georgian* for February 5, 1827 indicates a serious affair which occurred on the lightship after a crew member had had an argument with the captain: "Key West Captain Johnson spoke [with] the light ship *Caesar* on Carysfort Reef, the captain of which requested him to state that part of his crew had been in a state of mutiny and had broken his lantern, etc. but were then in irons [shackles]." Johnson alerted the United States Revenue Cutter Service (forerunner of the Coast Guard) about the problem. On April 13, 1827, Key West Collector of Customs William Pinkney reported to Stephen Pleasonton that the insubordinate man had "been Sent to St. Augustine to be tried." However, he was returned, for the May 14, 1827, issue of the *Savannah Georgian* reports: "Key West The [U. S. Revenue Cutter] *Marion*, [Captain] Doane, looked into this harbor last week, and landed a seaman from the light ship as a prisoner under a charge of mutiny; he having refused, as is said, to obey the order of the keeper, and also during his absence broke the lamp and the bell."[3]

Pinkney reported to Stephenson that during the month of March, 1827, the lightship was undergoing extensive caulking and repair; however, later, in a storm that fall, the lightship was blown onto the reef, damaging the copper sheathing of her hull. By July, 1828, damage to the lightship from its exposure to the elements was becoming apparent. Captain Whalton wrote a letter to Pinkney, from the "Light Ship *Cesar*," describing the problems he found with the vessel. Whalton wrote: "Her Plank Sheer is entirely rotten, there are three planks on the starboard bow, two on the larboard bow, and seven bad places under each tuck which cannot be caulked." Because the copper sheathing on the bottom had been damaged when the vessel was blown onto the reef, teredo worms had gotten into the wooden hull, and it was badly eaten out.

In August, 1828, Pleasonton authorized Pinkney to have the lightship taken into port and repaired. Notice of the vessel's removal from her station, though, had to be advertised, "and also when she shall be repaired and replaced." In October, when the light vessel was finally brought into Key West for repairs, it was learned that the damage was much more severe than originally thought, and the vessel was sent to Charleston for major rebuilding. After a complete survey, it was discovered that the main timbers of the ship were already so rotted that repair of the vessel was not deemed economical. The final fate of the *Ceasar*, the first Carysfort Reef lightship, has not been discovered, but being rotted, she was probably broken up.

By the middle of 1828, it was obvious that the lightship at Carysfort Reef would have to be replaced. As Stephen Pleasonton reported:

> The decay of the first light vessel built for Carysfort Reef was very extraordinary and unaccountable. She was built in New York by Henry Eckford, under the superintendence of an experienced shipbuilder, and examined by the collector...I saw the vessel myself after her timbers were up, but before she was planked; and every other person who saw her, pronounced her a very superior vessel in every respect...[yet] in five years she was examined and found so entirely dry-rotten, in every timber, that a new vessel was found to be necessary to take her place.

In the spring of 1830, Congress authorized the construction of a new "vessel for a floating light" for Carysfort Reef. The contract was completed on June 3rd with Isaac Webb and John Allen of New York for $19,730. The new 225-ton vessel was christened *Florida*, and she reached her station the following summer, with Captain Whalton again in command.[4] However, conditions were not much improved over what they had been on board the old *Caesar*, and on September 15-17, 1835, the new light vessel was damaged in a hurricane.[5]

A new problem arose: Indian hostilities! The Second Seminole Indian War began with an Indian raid on New Smyrna and on the lighthouse at Mosquito Inlet on Christmas Day, 1835, and the massacre of Major Dade and his command three days later. The January 6, 1836, massacre of the Cooley family at New River, at today's Fort Lauderdale, brought the war closer to home for those in the Florida Keys. Twelve year old Edmund Kirby-Smith, later a famous Confederate general, traveling from St. Augustine to Key West, wrote to his mother that the sailors on the lightship were "alarmed for their safety." On July 23, 1836, the Indians attacked the Cape Florida Lighthouse, killing one keeper, wounding the other, and setting fire to the tower.[6] This left the men on the Carysfort Reef lightship the closest American outpost to the territory overrun by the Indians.

During the next year, however, things in the immediate area seemed to have quieted down so much that Captain Whalton invited his family from Key West to come up to the light vessel for a visit. To provide a special treat for them, on June 26, 1837, Whalton decided to go ashore on Key Largo. Here the men had cultivated a vegetable garden to supplement their meager provisions from Key West.[7] With the captain went four other men from the lightship. The men anticipated no trouble, but the Indians had been waiting for the lightship men to land. What happened was reported from Indian Key in the *Pensacola Gazette*:

Captain Whalton and one of his men were shot dead — the other three made their escape, two of which were wounded, one on the left side, the other in the arm. The Indians after taking scalps, stripped the bodies entirely naked and stabbing them in several places, even cutting off Captain Whalton's finger to get his ring, retreated to the bush. The wreckers, or several of them, deserve much credit. In the afternoon of the same day they resolved to go on shore to the risk of their own lives and get the bodies, and Capt. Cold of the Schooner *Pee Dee*, Capt. English on board the sloop *Brilliant* with their crews, ventured and got the remains, which were brought to this place [Indian Key] the next day, and as decently interred as circumstances would permit. The distressed family also came down and remained one night and took the Mail Packet for Key West.[8]

The attack on the men from the lightship *Florida* and the death of the popular Captain Whalton shocked everyone, and the entire Florida Keys were in a panic. Extra troops were stationed near Indian Key, but on August 7, 1840, even the large settlement on Indian Key was attacked and destroyed. At length, however, the Indian war was over.

Francis Watlington was appointed captain of the *Florida* after the death of John Whalton, and somehow, the vessel was kept in order despite the difficult exigencies of the times. After only two months, however, Watlington resigned, to be succeeded by William Neve. He resigned after a while, and a Captain Kimmer took his place. In 1841, Kimmer was removed and William Sistaire became captain. The following year, Joseph Ximenez (written "Himmenez" in some accounts), former keeper at the Dry Tortugas Lighthouse took over, and on October 22, 1846, Charles M. Johnson became captain.

After the war was over, people again began to look objectively at the lightship. Many ship captains, including M. D. Ricker, W. Rollins, and David Dixon Porter, complained that although the lightship was supposed to be displaying two flashing white lights fifty and sixty feet above the sea, visible for twelve miles, the lights were "scarcely discernible from the outer ridge of Carysfort reef, which is four to five miles distant." The captain of the mail-passenger steamer *Isabel*, making twice-monthly voyages between Charleston and Key West, called the Carysfort Reef lightship "a poor thing...cannot depend on it at all."

As early as 1837, Congress had authorized the building of a lighthouse at Carysfort Reef, complete with an appropriation of $20,000. However, the sum was too small to build the required lighthouse on the reef, and the Indian troubles made work in the Keys too dangerous at that time. On July 7, 1838, Congress added $40,000 to the appropriation, and Isaiah W. P. Lewis, a nephew of Winslow Lewis, drew the plans of a granite lighthouse designed by his uncle. But again, the Indian scare prevented work from being started.

In 1848, the effort was renewed, and this time, Isaiah W. P. Lewis designed an iron-pile lighthouse for the reef. The lightship *Florida* was to remain on station until the new lighthouse was completed. The lighthouse was assembled at its manufacturing plant in Philadelphia and then disassembled and shipped to Carysfort Reef. When the engineer in charge of construction died, Lt. George Gordon Meade, who eleven years later would lead Union troops to victory in the Civil War Battle of Gettysburg, was selected to complete the tower. The erection of the tower on the reef, however, proved to be more difficult than anticipated, and it was not until March 10, 1852, that the light was finally lit for the first time. Charles M. Johnson, captain of the *Florida*, was appointed the first keeper of the new lighthouse. A Captain Watlington arrived to sail the old light vessel away for the last time. The fate of this lightship is not presently known, but considering that the *Florida* manned the Carysfort Reef station for twenty-one years, the vessel was probably worn out beyond further use.

The Northwest Passage Lightship (1838-1855):
Key West

As Key West developed, more and more commerce began flowing into the city. It was discovered that the quickest way for ships with drafts of less than 12 feet to go from the Gulf of Mexico to Key West was by the way of the Northwest Passage. This seven-mile long route saved a vessel the dangerous and more circuitous course around the Dry Tortugas. On January 1, 1834, the "Residents of Key West" sent a Petition to Congress requesting that a lighthouse be erected at the outer entrance of the Northwest Passage. Realizing that the construction of a lighthouse at the Northwest Passage might be sometime away, Lt. Napoleon L. Coste, commanding the Revenue Cutter *Campbell*, suggested an alternative. He felt that when a new lighthouse was built at Carysfort Reef, "the light-boat [at Carysfort] may, if deemed practicable, be removed to the northwest bar of Key West."

However, even before the new lighthouse on Carysfort Reef could be built, Congress, on March 3, 1837, appropriated $10,000 for the construction of a "light boat" to be placed at the outer end of the Northwest Passage. In November, Stephen Pleasonton reported that advertisements for building the new lightship had been issued and that the vessel should be completed before June 1, 1838. On November 28th, William Easby received the contract for building the "vessel for a floating light."[9]

The 145-ton light vessel for the station at the Northwest Passage was completed in the summer of 1838 and sent to her station early that fall with three crew members under Jeremiah Cottrell, her first captain. The vessel displayed a single, small "fixed, white" light at its masthead, and it was claimed that it could be seen twelve nautical miles to sea. Although everyone seemed glad that this important entrance to Key West was finally marked, the Collector of Customs for Key West did have one complaint. In a letter of October 9, 1838, Adam Gordon reported to Captain Lawrence Rousseau that "The light-ship *Key West*, at the bar of the northwest channel leading to the gulf of Mexico, is a useful but feeble light, owing to the construction of its lamp. I have recommended to the Department to substitute a larger lamp with reflectors, showing more lights, &c. and have hopes it will soon be improved."

Captain Lawrence Rousseau, Naval lighthouse inspector for the Sixth District (Key West to the Sabine River, Texas) wrote Stephen Pleasonton agreeing with Gordon's recommendation. Although, "the light-boat *Key West*, at the bar of the northwest channel, is well placed and very useful," after new lamps would be installed, "nothing more will be required for the protection of navigation."[10] Although the vessel was only a few months old by December, 1838, Navy Lt. George N. Hollins, the lighthouse inspector for the Fifth Lighthouse District (Norfolk through Key West), reported that the "Northwest Passage Light-boat" was "not in very good order."

If only the vessel was the source of complaints, it would be bad enough, but then her captain got into trouble. With the new light vessel marking the channel, more and more ships began using the Northwest Passage. They needed pilots. Captain Cottrell of the *Key West* found himself at a location from which to take advantage of the new business and began taking "every vessel that comes that way," to the detriment of the other pilots. It was assumed that by being so employed, Cottrell might neglect his care of the lightship. Finally, in early 1840, Stephen Pleasonton ordered Cottrell to mind his duty and not to act again as a pilot. Although it appears that Cottrell followed his orders, he got into trouble again that year when it was learned that he had employed an under-aged youth on the vessel, 15-year-old John O'Brien. The lad was sent home.

Perhaps because of his troubles on the lightship but probably also as to escape the severe hot summer weather, in March, 1840, Captain Cottrell requested and received a leave of absence so that he could return to the north to tend to business matters. William Malcolm took over as commander of the lightship during April and May, when Peter Stout relieved him. Cottrell returned to the vessel in early December.

Jeremiah Cottrell resigned as captain of the lightship *Key West* on July 14, 1841, and Alexander L. Patterson succeeded him.[11] Captain Patterson may have wondered if he had made a mistake in taking the job when gale force winds, swinging up from the south for several days built up tremendously heavy seas. For two days unabated, the storm raged. It was hard work as the men struggled to keep the vessel on its station and manned the pumps.[12] In a short time, Captain Patterson resigned, and in March, 1842, Henry Benners became the new captain. That following September, Benners almost had a chance to experience his own hurricane on board the vessel, except that, fortunately for him, he was on shore leave at the time. This time, the storm lasted for four days and did considerable damage to the vessel. Customs Collector Adam Gordon soon reported that "The light-ship at the northwest bar has been brought in for repairs; and, on examining her copper, it was found so defective as to require new, which has been supplied; and she is moored today — having been thoroughly recaulked, recoppered, and repaired where needed."

In the fall of 1844, Captain Benners finally rode out his first hurricane on board the lightship *Key West.* The storm came up from Cuba and lashed the vessel during October 4th and 5th. Although half of Sand Key near Key West was blown away, the sturdy little vessel maintained her station without damage. However, on October 11th and 12th, 1846, one of most devastating storms to hit the Key West area swept through with terrible fury. Both the *Key West* and *Sand Key* lighthouses were completely swept away. As for the *Key West*, as Stephen Mallory, the Collector of Customs, reported, "during the storm, the lightship at Northwest Passage broke adrift from her moorings, but as her heavy chains kept her head into the wind and sea, she backed astern and drifted sixty miles to sea, safely...The light ship is now [October 21st] being moored at her station."

The old *Key West* had proved to be a sturdy and intrepid vessel, but complaints continued about the feebleness of her light. Although a report in *Hunt's Merchants' Magazine* acknowledged that the lightship was well kept, it again stressed the fact that the light on the ship was "by no means what it ought to be...the lightship is old and the light they attempt to show is miserable."

After the hurricane of 1846 had destroyed the Sand Key Lighthouse, a small, emergency light vessel was stationed off the remains of Sand Key until a new lighthouse could be built. During the summer of 1852, this vessel was removed from her station and sold. The new Lighthouse Board, which had just been instituted to replace Stephen Pleasonton in the charge of the nation's lighthouses, planned to move the *Key West* from the Northwest Passage to the now-vacant position at Sand Key. However, they received a report that the *Key West* was in critical condition herself and needed to be replaced. With the new Sand Key Lighthouse already under construction, the Light House Board finally decided that perhaps a lightship was not necessary at Sand Key and that the *Key West* should remain at the Northwest Passage. In debates, it was finally established that, in the long-run, a lighthouse at Northwest Passage would be much more cost-effective than maintaining the old light vessel.

In March, 1853, Congress appropriated $12,000 for the construction of an iron-pile, "house-style" lighthouse for Northwest Passage. In the meantime, the *Key West* was repaired and "restored to her position in an unusually short space of time, and at a mere nominal expense compared with what . . . it was supposed would be required."

In May, 1854, the pre-fabricated iron-pile foundation and the lighthouse dwelling arrived at the site. Because of the onset of the summer "sickly season," however, work could not resume until

October. The new lighthouse was not completed until March 5, 1855. Now the old light vessel *Key West* was no longer needed. For seventeen years this small vessel had braved the waves and storms of the Gulf of Mexico, guiding thousands of ships and vessels of all sizes into the port of Key West. After 1855, the old light vessel *Key West* fades away into the mists of history.

Lightship Key West *in a storm.*

The Sand Key Lightship (1847-1852):
Honey

On October 11, 1846, one of the most terrible hurricanes to hit the Florida Keys slammed into Key West. The lighthouses at both Key West and Sand Key were destroyed, and the lightship at the Northwest Passage had been blown sixty miles from its station. With no lighthouse now at the critical location of Sand Key, something had to be done very quickly to provide an aid to navigation.

To remedy the situation, Stephen Pleasonton quickly purchased a vessel of 140 tons in New York. This vessel was the *Honey*, and she was quickly converted into an emergency lightship. To man the vessel, Pleasonton had authorized a captain (at $700 per year), a mate (at $30 per month), a cook/steward (at $18 per month), six able-bodied seamen (at $15 per month), and an ordinary seaman (at $12 per month). The captain he first chose was Samuel Sanderson, but, for some reason, Sanderson declined. Pleasonton next turned to Joseph Ximenez, who had just retired from serving as the captain of the lightship *Florida* in October. Ximenez received his appointment on December 16, 1846.

The *Honey* sailed south to her station, carrying with her materials and even a pre-fabricated, frame dwelling house for re-building the new Key West Light Station on the Island of Key West. After off-loading this material in Key West, the new lightship took up her station southwest of the remains of Sand Key, where the new lighthouse would be built. This was a strategic location for the lightship as navigators could use it as a reference mark for entering the Rock Key Channel, the Southwest Channel, and the Main Ship Channel, all of which provided access to the harbor of Key West.

After five months as captain of the *Honey*, Ximenez stepped down, and on May 15, 1847, John Walker, formerly of Rhode Island, took over as captain. He would serve for two and a half years, and had some special adventures.

The Lighthouse Board encouraged its lighthouse keepers to assist mariners in distress as far as they were able. When George Gordon Meade completed the Carysfort Reef Lighthouse in 1852, he would instruct the keepers to "succor them [distressed mariners] as far as it is in [the keepers'] power whether by piloting or the supplying of sustenance or materials of any kind on hand." However, the wrecking court judge in Key West, William Marvin, saw this work by lighthouse men as a form of competition to the regularly licensed wreckers in Key West, and he worked to discredit their actions and discourage their participation in what he saw as the wrecking business and not the lighthouse business.

At midnight on a night in 1849, Captain John Walker sighted the light of a vessel in distress on the reef near the lightship. With four of his crew, he rowed out to offer assistance to the captain of the vessel which proved to be a schooner. Under the directions of the schooner's captain, Walker and his men used the schooner's boat to carry the vessel's kedge anchor out into the ocean to try to haul the schooner off the reef. When this smaller anchor failed to hold with enough force to pull the schooner off, Walker and his men rowed back to the vessel to get its much larger bower anchor out. However, in rowing this larger anchor out, its weight capsized the small boat. Walker and his men clung to the overturned hull of the boat, and then Walker swam back to the schooner, got another boat, and rowed back out to rescue his men. After towing the capsized boat and anchoring it off Sand Key, Walker and his men returned to the schooner and succeeded in heaving her free. Judge William Marvin was not amused when the lighthouse men came to the court in Key West to get their just dues for assisting the schooner. Marvin awarded the lighthouse men only $50 apiece for risking their lives.

In September, 1850, the *Honey* was brought into the port of Key West for an inspection. It had been thought that she was in bad condition, but the inspection found that her hull was sound enough to last another five years as a lightship. On November 19, 1850, William P. Courtland succeeded John Walker as captain of the lightship.

Many people complained of the ineffectiveness of the lightship. In 1850, John C. Hoyt, an insurance underwriter in Key West, complained that "the light-ship stationed near Sand Key is old and the light is miserable. Several vessels and much valuable cargo have been lost by the neglect of the government to build a lighthouse on Sand Key." Hoyt had figures to back up his assertions, for between May, 1850, and August, 1851, eight ships had run ashore near Sand Key with a loss of cargo valued at $425,000. He continued, "The three light-ships on this coast are faithfully kept, but the power of their lights is by no means what it should be." In August of 1851, the *Honey* was herself threatened with running ashore as a major hurricane struck the area. As the waves became higher and higher, and the vessel was threatened with destruction, Captain Courtland made the decision to slip his chains and run down into the harbor of Key West for safety.

In 1850 Isaiah Lewis, the architect of the Sand Key Lighthouse, had managed to install the foundation pilings and some stabilizing cross braces before the Congressional appropriation ran out. It was nearly two years before money again became available and George Gordon Meade was sent to complete the lighthouse. The funds, however, would not be available for recommencing the work until December. During the summer of 1852, while the lighthouse construction was thus in this state of hiatus, Sand Key had some unusual visitors, and the crew of the lightship had a ring-side seat to observe the situation. Jones Perry Fyffe, a gentleman who was returning home to Ohio from California and 170 fellow travelers spent a week on desolate Sand Key. Cholera had broken out on the ship on

which Fyffe was sailing, and when she sailed into Key West, authorities made her disembark her passengers on Sand Key until they could clear quarantine. Fyffe described the island as

> a small, barren island devoid of vegetation about one acre and a half in its extent. There is a lone frame house used by the government people [those who had been building the lighthouse]. A portion of our folks occupy it. The balance are scattered about, some under an awning stretched over the base of the new light house just commenced. The party to which I am attached are under a covered causeway used for landing the material for the light house.

The stranded people managed to create a shelter which worked fine until a squall a day later stirred things up and caused a small pilot boat to capsize and go adrift with a man aboard, clinging to it. Some fellows in another boat attempted to rescue him and were themselves blown away towards Key West. The man was finally rescued. The people tried and whipped a couple of men who had stolen some personal property, and several turtles were caught which made a fine stew. After several more days, twenty of the passengers charted a small pilot boat and headed off for Mobile.

Finally, after a week on Sand Key, Jones Fyffe and his fellow passengers were ferried back into Key West where they once again boarded their sanitized and completely repainted vessel to continue their voyage. It was an unpleasant stay on Sand Key for Jones Fyffe and his comrades, but for us, it is an interesting episode that occurred when the Sand Key Lighthouse was being built.

In September, 1852, the *Honey* was deemed unseaworthy and was removed from her station. The new Lighthouse Board, still in the throes of organization, planned to move the old *Key West* from the Northwest Passage to serve the Sand Key station. However, the *Key West* herself was in need of replacement. With the Sand Key Lighthouse now under construction and due to be completed in the next year, the Lighthouse Board finally decided that a lightship was no longer necessary at Sand Key. The *Key West* would remain at the Northwest Passage. The lightship *Honey* was sold and it vanished from the pages of history.

The history of these five tiny lightships and the brave crews who manned them is a testament to the tenacity of the men who served the early United States Lighthouse Establishment. Despite inferior equipment and technology, storms and Indian attacks, and despite the continuation of wrecks along the shores of the Florida Keys, these vessels and their crews should be accorded the accolades of having served their purpose, of having done their jobs, and having saved countless lives during their brief time on the treacherous coasts of the Florida Keys.

Part 2
Reef Lights of the Florida Keys

Introduction

The "Reef Lights" of the Florida Keys are the six major iron-pile lighthouses which mark the offshore reefs of the Florida Keys, stretching from Miami to Key West. During the nineteenth and twentieth centuries, these towers were essential for the safe navigation of the dangerous waters of the Keys and remain important beacons today for small boaters and fishermen. One of these lighthouses, the American Shoal Lighthouse off Sugarloaf Key, was featured on a United States postage stamp in 1990. As these lighthouses reflect engineering advances which affected the construction of lighthouses worldwide, two of the reef lights are (and the others should be) on the prestigious National Register of Historic Places. The lighthouses in the Keys are the largest assemblage of iron-pile lighthouses anywhere in the world. The iron construction used in these towers influenced Alexandre Gustave Eiffel to build his famous iron tower in Paris, France in 1889, which has become an international symbol for mankind. We could, therefore, call our iron towers "America's Eiffel Towers."

The iron-pile lighthouse originated in England with Alexander Mitchell who received the first patent for an iron-pile lighthouse design in 1833. The first such lighthouse was the Maplin Sand Lighthouse, built on a sandy shoal in the Thames estuary in 1841. The first iron-pile lighthouse authorized in the United States in 1847 was built at Minot's Ledge off the coast of Massachusetts. Although the structure was well-conceived, the engineer felt the extra bracing on the lower levels was unnecessary and omitted it. Because of this, the tower was blown over by a storm in 1850 with the loss of two keepers.

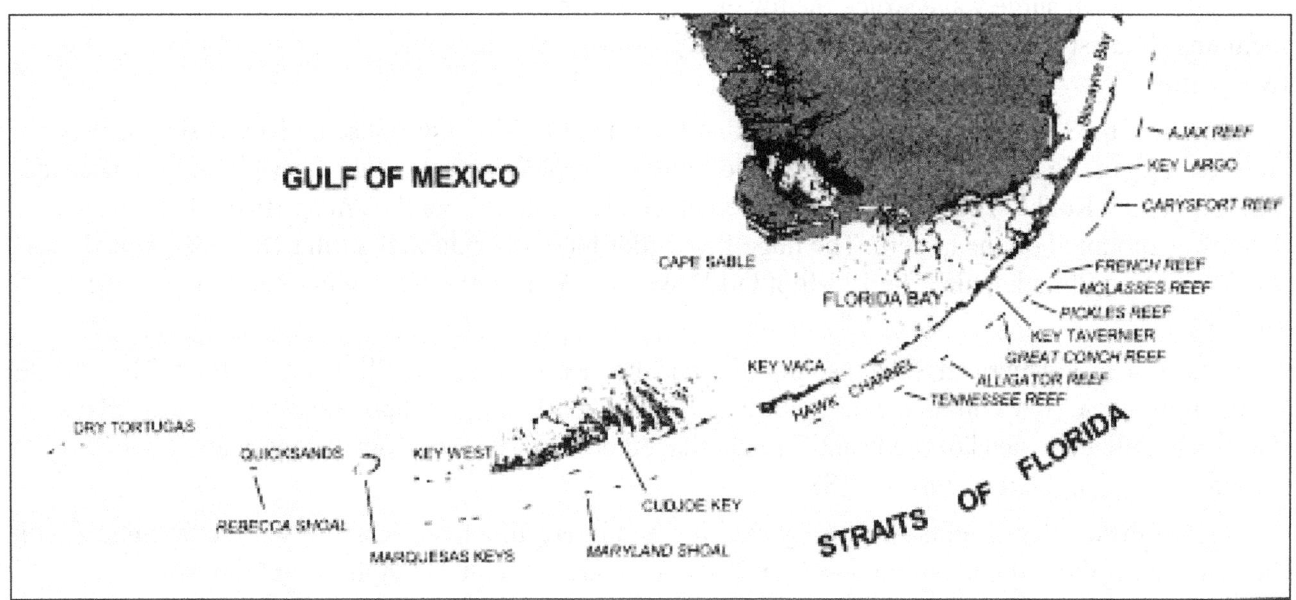

Reefs off the Florida Keys. Maryland Shoal is an error -- should read American Shoal.

In 1847, a lighthouse was also authorized for construction at Carysfort Reef in the Florida Keys. Winslow Lewis, a famous Boston lighthouse builder, designed a masonry tower for Carysfort, but the choice of a design was delayed until after the creation of the United States Lighthouse Board in 1852. Rather than use Winslow Lewis's tired old design, the new Board chose instead to use the revolutionary iron-pile design submitted by a nephew of Winslow Lewis, Isaiah W. P. Lewis, who had received Mitchell's patent in 1844 and his own patent from the United States in 1845.

A foundry in Philadelphia cast the iron skeletal structure for the new lighthouse and assembled it to make sure everything met specifications. Then, the tower was disassembled and shipped to Florida. As construction began, the engineer in charge died, and the Lighthouse Board sent Lt. George Gordon Meade to take charge. This 112-foot tall lighthouse at Carysfort Reef would be the first of three reef lights and four other lighthouses that Meade would build in Florida. The Carysfort Reef Lighthouse, the first reef light, began operation on March 10, 1852.

Meade's next task was to build the 132-foot tall Sand Key Lighthouse. The original lighthouse at this site, near Key West, had been a masonry tower built in 1826. It had been completely destroyed by a hurricane in 1846, and a lightship marked this site until a new lighthouse could be built. The new lighthouse would be an iron-pile lighthouse based on another design by Isaiah W. P. Lewis, but it had flanged plates on its foundation piles so that they could be screwed ten feet into the sand. This then, was the first "screw-pile" lighthouse. The Sand Key Lighthouse became operational on July 20, 1853.

The Lighthouse Board needed another lighthouse about half-way between the Carysfort Lighthouse off Key Largo, and the Sand Key Lighthouse off Key West, and in 1855, Meade began work on his third iron-pile lighthouse at Sombrero Key off Key Vaca (Marathon). However, on August 29, a hurricane blew down the temporary construction works there before the lighthouse could be built. In 1857, Meade started again, and the new lighthouse was successfully completed. The 156-foot tall Sombrero Key Lighthouse, the tallest of all the reef lights, began operation on March 17, 1858, and was the last iron-pile lighthouse in the Keys built by George Gordon Meade.

After the Civil War, the Lighthouse Board felt that additional reef lights were needed to safely guide the increasing commerce through the Florida Straits. The 136-foot Alligator Reef Lighthouse was completed on November 25, 1873. The Alligator Reef Lighthouse suffered perhaps the strongest of challenges of any of the reef lights when it was hit by the severe Labor Day Hurricane of 1935. A twenty-foot storm surge wave struck the tower, and the winds blew all of the glass out of the gallery, including the first-order Fresnel lens. For years afterwards, people would find prism fragments as far as twenty miles away on the shore.

In 1875, the Lighthouse Board decided that the Cape Florida Lighthouse on Key Biscayne was not close enough to the reefs to be an effective aid to navigation, therefore, a new iron-pile lighthouse was built on Fowey Rocks. The pilings were driven eleven feet into the coral. A magnificent bell-shaped dome was mounted on the lantern. The huge first-order lens was exhibited at the 1876 Centennial World's Fair in Philadelphia. The 125-foot tall Fowey Rocks Lighthouse began operation on June 15, 1878.

The 124-foot American Shoal Lighthouse was the last of the six reef lights to be built. The design for the lighthouse was a duplicate of the Fowey Rocks Lighthouse, but upon completion, a standard dome was utilized instead of the beautiful bell-shaped dome of Fowey Rocks. American Shoal Lighthouse was lighted on July 15, 1880.

All of these "Reef Lights" have very exciting and interesting histories. You will be fascinated with the histories of these unique lighthouses, and yes, there are even ghosts in these lighthouses!

The Eye Of Miami:
The Fowey Rocks Lighthouse

Because the reefs of the Florida Keys were so treacherous, Congress, in 1822, authorized the first lighthouses in Florida to be built at Cape Florida and in the Dry Tortugas to mark the ends of this very dangerous area. Although funding problems delayed the building of these towers, and St. Augustine and Pensacola had succeeded in getting their lighthouses built first, the lighthouse on Cape Florida was finally built and lit officially on March 10, 1825. Unfortunately, from its location on the south end of Key Biscayne, the Cape Florida Lighthouse, even with a second-order Fresnel lens, was not effective, as the lighthouse was still too far away from the reefs. When the first and second Cape Florida lighthouses had been built, the technology for building directly on the reefs had not yet existed. That would not come until the advent of the iron-pile lighthouses.

The United States Lighthouse Board knew that Cape Florida Lighthouse had to be replaced with an iron-pile structure directly on the reefs, but the Civil War intervened, and it was not until 1875 that Fowey Rocks was selected as the site for a new iron-pile lighthouse.

Fowey Rocks was another of those sections of the reef which seemed to stick out into the channel and snag ships. In fact, like so many other reefs, Fowey Rocks had been named for a shipwreck, that of the *HMS Fowey*, a 20-gun British sloop-of-war which had wrecked near there on June 27, 1748.

The design for this iron lighthouse was a new one, based on the iron construction used in the other reef lights, but with some Victorian touches, like moldings and a pseudo-French empire-style Mansard roof for the dwelling. The dwelling was two stories tall, with the first floor used primarily for machinery and the storage of supplies and the second floor used for living quarters for the keepers. The design of the lantern included a "bell-shaped" dome which had originally been designed in 1856. This would be its first incarnation. The Ponce de Leon Inlet Lighthouse near Daytona Beach would be the only other lighthouse in the United States to also use this beautiful and unique design. The Paulding and Kemble Company, of Cold Spring, New York, got the contract for building the iron foundation, and Pusey, Jones & Company of Wilmington, Delaware, got the contract for building the iron tower. The iron lantern and the first-order fixed Fresnel lens, made by the Henry-Lepaute firm of Paris, France, were displayed at the United States Centennial Exposition in Philadelphia in 1876.

Work began on the lighthouse in 1876, and Soldier Key, four miles away, was used as the depot for supplies and as the staging area for the work. An eighty-foot square platform was built at the reef site, and the workmen lived on the platform in tents. While the work was underway, two ships nearly ran down the platform but grounded on the reef just in time.

The Fowey Rocks Lighthouse was

Fowey Rocks Lighthouse

finished and lit for the first time on June 15, 1878. The keeper from the now-discontinued Cape Florida Lighthouse moved over to become the keeper of the new Fowey Rocks Lighthouse. The 125-foot lighthouse had cost $165,015 to build. Its daymark was "a brown octagonal, pyramidal skeleton tower enclosing white stair cylinder; octagonal dwelling with green trim and shutters." The focal plane height of its light above sea level was 110 feet.

Less than three months after completion, the lighthouse experienced its first hurricane. Fortunately, only minor structural damage occurred, the worst of which was the water leakage around the lantern windows which threatened to put out the light. Like that of the other reef lights, the history of the Fowey Rocks Lighthouse contains many stories of hurricanes, wrecks, rescue missions performed by the keepers, and various events in the lives of the keepers. One assistant keeper was Jefferson B. Browne. During his time on the lighthouse, he read a lot of history and studied law. He later wrote a history of Key West and became a judge of the Florida Supreme Court.

The lighthouse was so popular that the Lighthouse Board decided to feature it at the 1893 World's Columbian Exposition in Chicago with a model and a painting. By 1923, the lighthouse was equipped with a telephone. The telephone lines were contained in a submarine cable from Miami. This telephone was important in 1926 when the keepers were warned in advance of the terrible hurricane which hit Miami in that year. During the mid-1930s, the light was changed from incandescent oil vapor to electric power from generators installed on the first floor. At the same time, a radio beacon was erected on top of the lantern dome.

After the Coast Guard took over in 1939, the lighthouse became known as the "Eye of Miami," probably because it was the first light seen by ships approaching the city from the south. A four-man Coast Guard crew remained on the lighthouse until 1974, making this the last of the Florida Reef lights to be automated. As part of the automation of the light, the radio beacon was removed and relocated to the entrance of Miami harbor. In 1975, a windmill generator for batteries was tried but found not to be very successful. Solar panels were installed to charge the batteries. The first-order Fresnel lens was removed in 1982 and is on display today at the Coast Guard National Aids to Navigation School in Yorktown, Virginia.

In 1987 the lighthouse was repainted. A few years later, the Coast Guard removed unused water tanks that were located on the working platform underneath the dwelling. It was feared that the tanks would fall down in a storm and damage the foundation before they would break up.

In 1992, the Fowey Rocks Lighthouse was right in the path of Hurricane Andrew. Despite every pane of glass being blown out of the lantern, the lighthouse continued operation. Some people say that there is no need for lighthouses with the expanding use of the GPS navigation system. However, this writer knows better. A couple of years ago, he spoke with the first mate of a freighter which had lost all electrical power due to a lightning strike. No radio would work, and their navigation system had been completely destroyed. This first mate was the only person on board who could use a sextant, and with that sextant, he navigated the freighter to where he could see the Fowey Rocks Lighthouse. He admitted that without his sextant and that lighthouse, he was certain that their vessel would have crashed on the reefs and created an ecological disaster for the upper Keys. So lighthouses remain important, even if only as secondary and back-up navigational systems. Today, a state-of-the-art Vega VRB-25 optic is installed, and the lighthouse remains an active and very important aid to navigation into the Miami area. The light today flashes twice every ten seconds and contains two red sectors.

On clear days, the Fowey Rocks Lighthouse can be seen from the old Cape Florida Lighthouse on the southern tip of Key Biscayne. Lying inside Biscayne National Park, Fowey Rocks Lighthouse is surrounded by the reef which is about five feet deep at its shallowest. Just seaward of the lighthouse is a popular fishing area.

The Carysfort Reef Lighthouse: Oldest is Rich in History

On October 23, 1770, the British twenty-eight gun frigate HMS *Carysfort* grounded on a section of the Florida reefs off upper Key Largo near where the 60-gun ship of the line TMS (Their Majesties' Ship) *Winchester* had wrecked on September 24, 1695. The sailing master, Mr. Hunter, was able to get the *Carysfort* safely off the reef. This was clearly a very dangerous section of the Florida reefs. In 1771, less than a year after the grounding of the *Carysfort*, William Gerard de Brahm, King George III's Surveyor General for the Southern District of North America, completed his survey of the Florida Keys and noted the location of the *Carysfort*'s grounding on his official chart. He named the reef for the *Carysfort* on his chart.

In 1824, Congress appropriated $20,000 for a lightship to be anchored here to provide a navigational aid in this very dangerous section of the Florida reefs. The first lightship, the *Caesar* went on duty in 1826 but lasted only five years before becoming unserviceable due to rot. She was replaced in 1831 by the *Florida*. After the Seminole Indians attacked and put out of commission the Cape Florida Lighthouse in July, 1836, the lightship at Carysfort became an even more important aid to navigation.

Despite the lightship on Carysfort Reef, between 1833 and 1841, some sixty-three vessels still were lost on Carysfort Reef. Between January, 1844, and May, 1847, the value of the ships and cargoes wrecked on Carysfort Reef amounted to $650,000, making the wreckers of the Keys very rich.

In 1848, with maintenance of the lightship becoming exceedingly expensive and unreliable, Congress appropriated funds for the building of a permanent lighthouse at Carysfort Reef. A design for a traditional masonry tower was submitted by Winslow Lewis of Boston, one of the most noted lighthouse builders of his day. However, the

Carysfort Light

design selected for the new lighthouse at Carysfort Reef was an iron-pile design by Winslow Lewis' nephew, Isaiah W. P. Lewis. Although the fact that the skeletal structure of an iron-pile lighthouse would allow hurricane winds to blow through it without major damage was a major consideration which recommended this style of lighthouse for the Florida Keys, the deciding factor in the end was the fact that the iron-pile lighthouse would be considerably cheaper to build on a submerged site than the traditional masonry tower.

The I. P. Morris and Company foundry in Philadelphia got the contract for fabricating all of the iron parts for the new lighthouse. Soon, work on constructing the tower was begun under Captain Howard Stansbury of the Army Topographical Engineers. Captain Stansbury had served in Florida during the Second Seminole War and, in 1839, had had a fort named for him one mile north of Wakulla Springs in the Tallahassee area.

The foundation pilings for the Carysfort Reef Lighthouse were newly-designed with flanges on the bottom end which would screw down into the coral rock as the pilings were turned by horses on a platform above the water. However, the coral rock was not as solid as expected, being only a crust with softer, sandier material below, and the pilings were not steady enough. Stansbury devised a method of better securing the pilings by adding a round, eight-foot in diameter, iron "foot plate" around the base of the piling where it extended out of the coral. This invention of the "foot plate" proved to be critical to the building of the Florida reef lights and has helped to ensure their durability against many hurricanes.

Work on the lighthouse was now delayed by financial lapses, and when funding finally resumed, Captain Stansbury was out west fighting Indians. Major Thomas B. Linnard was sent to continue the work, but he soon died. Lt. George Gordon Meade was then sent to complete the work. Meade had served in Florida in the Second Seminole War and as an engineer on railroad building projects. For the government, he had surveyed the boundary between the United States and Texas, and he had helped to build a screw-pile lighthouse in the Delaware Bay. Meade would later become more famous as the Union general who defeated Robert E. Lee at the Civil War battle at Gettysburg. Unhappily, as Meade struggled to complete the lighthouse, funds again ran out, and it was not until March 10, 1852, that the lighthouse was finally finished. The new iron-pile lighthouse stood 112 feet tall and enclosed a two-story keeper's dwelling on its lower levels. The foundation piles of the lighthouse were painted black, with the upper piles and dwelling painted red. The doors and windows of the dwelling were white. As the new first-order Fresnel lens which had been purchased for this lighthouse was inexplicably sold, Meade had installed 18 old reflector lamps for the light. On March 10, 1852, the new principal keeper, Charles M. Johnson, a former captain of the Carysfort lightship, lit the light at the top of the lighthouse for the first time. The Carysfort Reef Lighthouse would not get its magnificent first-order revolving Fresnel lens until 1855. That lens today is on display at the Historical Museum of Southern Florida in Miami, and is one of the most magnificent lighthouse lenses in the United States.

Although most of the official records for the Carysfort Reef Lighthouse were destroyed in a Commerce Department fire in 1921, other records and letters provide some great stories of the keepers and the storms and shipwrecks they faced. In 1942, the 300-foot freighter *Benwood* was lost nearby, damaged by collision with another ship and sunk by gunfire from a submarine.

In 1913, an incandescent vapor oil lamp was installed in the lighthouse, and in 1962, it was electrified and automated. The first-order lens was removed in 1962 and was replaced with a third-order lens. This second lens was removed in 1982 and is now on display in the officers' mess at the Coast Guard Station, Miami Beach. A series of modern optics have been used in the Carysfort Reef Lighthouse, and today, the light is provided by a Vega VRB-25 Rotating Beacon. Recent plans to use the lighthouse as a marine laboratory under the auspices of the National Oceanographic and Atmospheric Administration (NOAA) and the Pennekamp Coral Reef Institute have not materialized, but this lighthouse remains as the oldest lighthouse of its kind in operation in the United States and is one of the two reef lights listed on the National Register of Historic Places.

Alligator Reef Lighthouse:
Survivor of the 1935 Hurricane

By 1860, the United States Lighthouse Board had made great progress in its efforts to "light the Keys" and make this area safer for commercial navigation. The three great, revolutionary iron-pile lighthouses at Carysfort Reef, Sand Key, and Sombrero Key were the engineering marvels of the lighthouse world and were featured in numerous newspapers and magazines around the world. However, the Lighthouse Board recognized that there were still some major "dark" areas and that further lighthouses were needed between Carysfort Reef and Sombrero Key and between Sombrero Key and Sand Key. However, the War Between the States intervened and postponed the Board's great lighthouse building efforts.

After the Civil War, the Lighthouse Board resumed their plans to fill in the gaps, with the top priority to place a lighthouse on Alligator Reef off the southern end of Upper Matecumbe Key. This had long been known as a dangerous area and was named for the 12-gun naval schooner USS *Alligator*, which had wrecked here on the night of November 19, 1822. Her recently-deceased captain, Lt. William Howard Allen, mortally wounded while fighting pirates off Matanzas, Cuba, a few days earlier, would be honored when the new settlement on Key West was named Allentown. This name, however, did not stick, but the reef on which his ship died would retain his ship's name.

Ill-fated USS Alligator

Many other ships shared the *Alligator's* fate on its namesake reef. On June 2, 1846, the *St. Augustine Florida Herald* reported: "The mail packet *Stranger* on her way from Key West to this port, reported a large ship...ashore on Alligator Reef. This is an extremely dangerous point of navigation, which is not indicated by any light. The current of the Gulf Stream sweeps directly upon this reef . . . and it is a very easy thing for even the most prudent navigator, with his lead line constantly going, to find himself suddenly upon the rocks." In 1852, Lt. James Totten of the U. S. Army Coast Survey, installed a screw-pile day beacon on Alligator Reef by placing a black barrel on top of a 32-foot tall iron post. This marker could be seen in the daytime for two to three miles, but this was certainly not adequate. In 1857, the Lighthouse Board recommended that an iron-pile lighthouse be built on Alligator Reef.

For several years after the Civil War, the Lighthouse Board had sought funding for the lighthouse, and finally, on July 15, 1870, Congress gave in and appropriated funds for a lighthouse on the reef. Nearby Indian Key was selected as the staging area for the lighthouse construction. The Lighthouse

Alligator Reef Lighhouse

Board had been so impressed with George Gordon Meade's design for the Sombrero Key Lighthouse that the design for the new lighthouse on Alligator Reef would be a near duplicate. For ease of construction, efficiency of design, and economy, this design could not be topped for a lighthouse built on the reefs.

In 1871, workmen descended on Indian Key and built "a new wharf, quarters for the mechanics and laborers…a capacious cistern, a smithery, and a large shed for the iron-work and other materials for the lighthouse, whence it can be transported as wanted to the reef." The men also built a fuel wharf and an adjoining coal storage building. Paulding Kemble of Cold Springs, New York, forged the iron-pile structure and shipped it to Indian Key.

At the construction site on the northeast end of Alligator Reef, workmen sank mangrove pilings five feet into the coral and built a landing jetty and a construction platform. Then, the cast-iron foundation disks, or "foot plates," had to be set in an octagonal pattern, fifty-six feet in diameter, on the bottom in five feet of water. As a Lighthouse Board report stated: "By an ingenious system of gauges, the disks were set into their positions, with their proper relative distances." A portable steam-operated pile driver with a 2,000 pound hammer, then drove the 12-inch diameter, 26-foot long piles through the center of the foundation disks, ten feet into the coral. Everything had to be precision-set before the pilings could be joined by cross-braces and the second set of pilings installed.

As the lighthouse began to reach into the sky as successive sets of pilings were added, delays were experienced from inclement weather and from the Congressional funding running out. Congress finally appropriated an additional $25,000, and the work was completed. A first-order Fresnel lens from France was installed, giving the lighthouse a flashing signal with five white flashes and the sixth, red. The light was first exhibited on November 25, 1873. The focal plane height of the light above sea level was 136 feet, and the light could be seen for eighteen nautical miles. The lighthouse, painted a brilliant white with a black lantern to be seen far at sea during the day, had cost $185,000.

As with many of the reef lights in the Keys, there are many storms and shipwrecks in the history of the Alligator Reef Lighthouse, but this lighthouse remained a favorite of the Lighthouse Board. In 1893, the Alligator Reef Lighthouse was represented in a painting at the Lighthouse Board's exhibit at the Columbian World's Fair Exposition in Chicago. In its brochure, the Lighthouse Board wrote: "This is one of the finest and most effective lights on the Coast," and "one of the most gracefully designed iron-pile structures in the Keys."

For most of the lighthouses in the Keys, no light station journals exist due to destruction by hurricanes; however, some light station journals from the Alligator Reef Lighthouse do still exist. An entry from January 31, 1929, tells of the keepers seeing President Herbert Hoover fishing off the lighthouse. The President was an avid fisherman and came to the Keys several times. Alligator Reef was his favorite fishing spot.

The journal entry of September 2, 1935, however, tells of something more ominous: the great Labor Day Hurricane. This category 5 hurricane smashed into Alligator Reef Lighthouse and the Matecumbe Keys with 200 mph winds. The barometer at the lighthouse read 27.35 inches, one of the lowest readings ever taken in the United States. The keeper wrote:

6:30 P.M. while lighting the Lamp for the night, the lantern glass began to break; red sectors began to break; flying glass was danger to Life. I left the watch room and hurried to living quarters; the doors began to break in. The keeper's and second assistant's rooms was badly damaged to doors, and water soaked beds and clothing. I managed to save the doors in the first assistant's room and the kitchen. The lens was completely wrecked and other damage [was] done by wind and water to the watch room and the property there. The Row boat washed away about 8 P.M. The launch no. 34 was in fair condition at 9:30 P.M. This was the last time we were able to be outside until the next day. The platform landing was completely wrecked, and launch no. 34 gone. This is the worst hurricane I have experienced, during the eleven years of service. The light will be out of commission until temporarily repaired.

[Signed by] Jones A. Pervis, Rating Keeper.

On land, the Overseas Railway was wrecked, and nearly every house in the Matecumbes was flattened. Over 700 people lost their lives. A few days later, an enclosed lightship lantern was installed in the lantern of the Alligator Reef Lighthouse until the lantern glass and another optic could be installed. In the case of a small miracle, one glass prism from a lower panel of the huge first-order lens was blown out of the lantern more than four miles to land on a beach without the fragile glass shattering. A passerby later found it, and today, this unique and rare piece of the destroyed Alligator Reef Lighthouse lens is in the collection of historian Jerry Wilkinson of Tavernier.

The Lighthouse went through Hurricane Donna in 1960. During this storm, the keepers lashed themselves to the framing of the structure to keep from being blown away. After the storm, one keeper wrote: "We looked out and saw a sight we will never forget if we live a thousand years. Scattered over the ocean, like croutons on a dish of soup, were derelict small boats, pieces of boats, chairs, bedsteads, boxes, lumber, trash, rising and falling on a twelve foot sea that still ran frothy and gray."

In June, 1963, the lighthouse was automated, so no one had to be aboard during the hurricane of 1965. The Alligator Reef Lighthouse remains today an important and active aid to navigation, and a modern, New Zealand-made Vega VRB-25 rotating beacon optic shines forth.

Sombrero Key Lighthouse

Sombrero Key Lighthouse:
Active Aid to Navigation

In the 1850s the Lighthouse Board had replaced the old, rotting Carysfort Reef lightship with an iron skeletal tower, and it had replaced the fallen, masonry tower at Sand Key with another iron tower. Now, it was time to place a lighthouse between these two lights, somewhere near Key Vaca. The new tower would be about 160 feet tall, the tallest of the lighthouses yet built in the Florida Keys.

In 1854, newly-promoted Captain George Gordon Meade was again chosen to build a new lighthouse, and this one, he would design himself. Although a primitive red and white barrel-on-a-pole day-beacon had been erected on nearby Sombrero Key in 1852, the initial location for the new lighthouse was on a reef known as Coffin's Patch, some nine miles east of Sombrero Key.

The I. P. Morris and Company of Philadelphia got the contract from the Lighthouse Board for all the ironwork for the new lighthouse. The wrought-iron tower would be assembled in Philadelphia to make sure everything fit together perfectly, then disassembled and shipped. In the summer of 1856, temporary construction works were built at Coffin's Patch in preparation for erecting the new lighthouse. Meade felt sure the lighthouse could be finished by the end of the year. However, on August 29, 1856, his hopes were dashed as a major hurricane swept the area and destroyed the construction works at Coffin's Patch. With the current Congressional funding nearly expended, Meade used the halt in construction to search for a better place for the new lighthouse. He found it on a barely submerged island called Dry Banks locally, but officially known as Sombrero Key. This was an important area to mark, for Sombrero Key once had been a low, dangerous sandy island but now was a series of even more dangerous shallow coral reefs, invisible to mariners until they were on top of them.

The lighthouse materials were ready for shipment, and Congress had appropriated more funds, but Meade delayed construction on the lighthouse until the nine 12-inch in diameter iron foundation piles could be galvanized. The process cost an additional $10,000, but Meade felt sure that such treatment would allow these most important piles to last for 200 years before eroding to the point where structural integrity might be compromised. He was right, and the Lighthouse Board concurred. In 1857, when the piles arrived, Meade finally started building the lighthouse on Sombrero Key.[13]

Meade sank the foundation piles through eight-foot diameter "foot pads" ten feet into the coral rock. Eight piles formed the shape of an octagon, 56 feet in diameter, with the final pile driven in the center. Each pile could support an estimated 64 tons. Six more sets of piles were built on top of the foundation, as the tower tapered from 56 feet wide at the base to 15 feet wide at the top. A 350 foot square keepers' dwelling was built within the second set of piles. The dwelling was constructed of one-quarter inch boiler plate and contained 4 rooms with wood interior walls. From the center of the keepers' dwelling, a stair column with 133 steps led upwards to the lantern.

With the lighthouse structure completed, it was time to install the lens. Since the Carysfort Reef and Sand Key lighthouses had flashing characteristics, it was decided to put a fixed light in the Sombrero Key Lighthouse. The first-order Fresnel lens was made by the firm of L. Sautter and Company in Paris and cost the Lighthouse Board $20,000. This was only the second such lens installed in a Florida lighthouse. In installing the lamp inside the lens, Meade used some subterfuge. He initially installed the typical French carcel lamp which was standard equipment. This was the lamp which Keeper Joseph Bethel and his assistants lighted when the lighthouse went into operation on March 17, 1858. Meade let the keepers use this lamp for five nights. Then, he changed the lamp. He installed a new hydraulic lamp of his own design. The keepers were so impressed with the ease of the new lamp's operation and its efficiency that they could hardly believe it. Their strong recommendation helped get George Gordon Meade's new lamp adopted by the United States government as its new standard. It would remain the American lamp of choice until a new fuel, kerosene, required a different kind of lamp. George Gordon Meade's new lamp had its national debut at the Sombrero Key Lighthouse.

With a focal plane height of 142 feet above sea level, and an overall height of 156 feet, the Sombrero Key Lighthouse is the tallest reef light in the Florida Keys. Meade had estimated the cost at $118,405.60, but due to the damage caused by the hurricane and other contingencies, the actual cost had come to $153,158.81.

Service aboard the Sombrero Key Lighthouse was a very remote duty in the early days, since the nearest large settlement was Key West. Families were not allowed to live in the tight quarters of the reef lights, and it took a very special breed of men to stand the constant tedium of the loneliness. It also could be dangerous work, and four men lost their lives at the Sombrero Key Lighthouse. [See Part 3, "Lost Keepers of Sombrero Key Lighthouse."]

The reefs around Sombrero Key Lighthouse were so treacherous that in the 1890s red sectors were added to the lantern to provide a red light over the most dangerous sections of the reef. These red sectors remain in the lighthouse today, giving the lighthouse a red flashing light when viewed from certain areas. In 1912, the kerosene wick-lamp was replaced with an incandescent oil vapor (IOV) lamp.

In 1939, the Coast Guard assumed the charge of all of the nation's lighthouses, but the duties did not change much. During World War II, the lights were maintained, and the task of watching for enemy submarines was added to the keepers' duties.

Through the years, the keepers at Sombrero Key Lighthouse suffered the travail of many storms. During Hurricane Donna in 1960, 128 mile-per-hour winds kicked up 12 to 20 foot seas which smashed into the lower platform of the lighthouse and carried away the station's fuel tanks and work shop. The Coast Guard keepers were able to save the station's boat, but it was too damaged for them to use to get ashore. Finally, after the storm, local fishing boats brought the keepers in to Vaca Cut, where the only structure they saw standing was the first floor of a two story building. The men swore that they would never return to the lighthouse, but they did. However, they were not there for long, because later that year, the Coast Guard automated the lighthouse. In 1982, the original first-order Fresnel lens, which had served for 124 years, was removed by the Coast Guard. It is now on display at the Key West Lighthouse Museum. The lens was replaced by an experimental flash-tube array optic. This system did not work as well as hoped, and it was soon replaced by a solar-charged flashing 300 mm optic. Later, a solarized, 190 mm rotating beacon was installed.

In 1997, a 12-volt, 25-inch Vega VRB-25 rotating beacon was installed. In the past couple of years, a Radar Beacon (RACON) has been installed. This special radar responder device returns to vessels a Morse Code radar signal which identifies the lighthouse, so now the lighthouse has not only a special daymark (red-brown skeletal tower), a special night characteristic, group flashing of five flashes each minutes, but also a special radar signal. The Sombrero Key Lighthouse remains today an active aid to navigation.

American Shoal Lighthouse:
The Lonely Lighthouse

After the Fowey Rocks Lighthouse had begun operation in 1878 there was only one hole left in the Lighthouse Board's plan to light the reef of the Florida Keys with a lighthouse about every twenty-five miles apart. This last hole was between Sombrero Key and Sand Key.

At first, the Lighthouse Board decided to build the new lighthouse on Looe Key, about six miles south of Ramrod Key. Looe Key was originally an actual low, sandy island which was named for the HMS *Loo*, a British 44-gun frigate which wrecked there on February 5, 1744.

In January, 1826, the U. S. government completed a 30-foot tall whitewashed brick tower, surmounted by a large black iron ball, on the small sandy island. [See the Appendix, "Trying to Build a Beacon on Looe Key."] This unlighted day-beacon tower was so prominent that navigators occasionally mistook it for the Key West Lighthouse. To solve this problem, a 10-foot tall red stripe was painted around the middle section of the white tower to alter its appearance and make it look different from the all-white tower on Whitehead Point on Key West. Unhappily, on October 1, 1833, a hurricane eroded away the foundation, and the Looe Key beacon collapsed. A second tower was contracted for, but before it could be built, the island washed away completely. Through the years, simpler, pole day-beacons were erected here, and the Lighthouse Board had thought about replacing the last one with the next iron-pile lighthouse. However, in 1876, the Lighthouse Board decided that American Shoal was "more nearly the desired position." The need for a navigational marker on American Shoal had been recognized as early as 1852, when a thirty-six-foot-high iron screw pile was erected, topped by a red hooped lattice-work, as a day marker.

American Shoal Lighthouse

On June 20, 1878, Congress appropriated $75,000 for the building of a lighthouse on American Shoal. The Lighthouse Board had already surveyed the four acres of underwater property which the State of Florida then transferred to the Federal government. The Lighthouse Board would use the plans for Fowey Rocks Lighthouse to build a duplicate for American Shoal. The only difference would be in the lantern, which omitted the bell-shaped dome for a less costly and more traditional one.

The Phoenix Iron Works of Trenton, N.J., got the $47,000 contract for the iron work. The tower was preassembled and disassembled in Trenton before it was shipped to Key West in 1879. Good weather during the winter of 1879-1880 allowed the lighthouse to be built quickly. In its lantern was installed a revolving, flashing first-order Fresnel lens made by the Henry-Lepaute Company of Paris, France. This flashing light would contrast with the fixed lights on either side of it at the Sand Key and Sombrero Key lighthouses. For a daymarker, the lighthouse structure and keepers' dwelling were painted brown, the stair column was painted white, and the lantern was black. Although the Fowey Rocks Lighthouse and American Shoal are nearly twin structures, this color scheme made them appear different. The 124-foot tall American Shoal Lighthouse was completed and first lighted on July 15, 1880. American Shoal would be the last of the six reef lights to be built.

In 1912, American Shoal Lighthouse received an I.O.V. lamp. Red sectors, to provide a red light out over the reefs, were also installed. In the 1920s crystal radio sets were installed in the lighthouses. After the 1926 hurricane, a keeper's family in Miami asked that news of their survival be broadcast so that the keepers out on the Fowey Rocks Lighthouse would know that their families were safe. However, not all of the lighthouses had radios to receive such news. Hearing about this, in 1931, a Key West woman donated radio sets as Christmas presents to the keepers at American Shoal, Sombrero Key, Alligator Reef, and Carysfort Reef. The Atwater-Kent Number 82 sets, complete with batteries and antennae, were delivered by the lighthouse tender *Ivy*.

The American Shoal Lighthouse was automated in June, 1963. Extensive repairs were made in 1980 when American Shoal, Sombrero Key, and Alligator Reef lighthouses were slated to be used as radar/visual stations during the Mariel refugee exodus from Cuba. From July through November, 1980, six Coast Guardsmen lived on the American Shoal Lighthouse. The Coast Guard said that the lighthouse had "great potential in our mission to protect lives and property and in the enforcement of federal laws."

Despite the lighthouse, wrecks and groundings have continued. In 1983, the 89-foot shrimp boat *Cleo* struck the reef. In August, 1994, the University of Miami's research vessel *Columbus Iselin* crunched four major coral formations on nearby Looe Key. The University paid $200,000 in fines to the federal government.

In the 1980s the first-order Fresnel lens was removed and shipped to the Coast Guard's National Aids to Navigation School in Yorktown, Virginia. In recent months, the lens has been uncrated, and it is now in the process of restoration by volunteers of the Chesapeake Bay Chapter of the United States Lighthouse Society. Today, as in all of the reef lights, a Vega VRB-25 rotating beacon is in place to provide the flashing light. Also now in place is the new RAdar beaCON or RACON, by which radar signals are reflected with a Morse Code signal which identifies each radar contact.

The American Shoal Lighthouse seems to be the loneliest of the reef lights. Dive shops on Key Biscayne visit the reefs around Fowey Rocks Lighthouse, dive shops on Key Largo carry divers out to the spectacular reefs around the Carysfort Reef Lighthouse. The case is the same for the Alligator Reef, Sombrero Key, and Sand Key lighthouses. However, American Shoal Lighthouse seems to be in that part of the Keys which is yet relatively undeveloped, and the divers in this area go to the closer and more spectacular reefs at Looe Key. Thus, it is more likely for one to visit American Shoal Lighthouse with no one else around. Sometimes, a small private fishing boat might be on the good fishing grounds of American Shoal, but for the most part, this reef light is visited far more infrequently than any of the others. Nevertheless, the American Shoal Lighthouse has the distinction of being the only reef light to have appeared on a United States postage stamp. The stamp bearing the image of this lighthouse was part of the American lighthouse postage stamp series, issued on April 26, 1990. The stamp does, however, have a couple of errors. It misspelled the name of the lighthouse by making the name, American Shoal, plural, and it shows a 210-foot Coast Guard cutter passing close to the lighthouse in an area which is only five feet deep, a feat which could not be duplicated in real life without a nice wreck! So much for artistic license.

Although remote and difficult to get to without your own boat, the American Shoal Lighthouse can be seen from shore. From the intersection with Sugarloaf Boulevard on Sugarloaf Key, where the Sugarloaf Lodge is on the north side of U.S. 1, turn south and follow Sugarloaf Boulevard (State Route 939) for 5.2 miles to a small concrete bridge near the end of the road. From this bridge is the best land view of American Shoal Lighthouse. Even from this vantage point, a good set of binoculars are essential to see this lighthouse.

The Sand Key Lighthouse

The United States Lighthouse Board had wanted to light the Florida reefs with a lighthouse approximately every twenty-five miles. This would allow a ship at sea to be within the range of the navigation light of a major lighthouse almost constantly as it sailed past the dangerous reefs. However, in the 1850s it seemed that the Lighthouse Board was playing catch-up. It had to first replace the old, rotting lightship at Carysfort Reef, and then it had to build a new lighthouse to replace the one at Sand Key.

The small islet known as Sand Key has always been important for navigation to Key West Harbor. In the 1770s British surveyor George Gauld erected a pole day-beacon on the island, and in the early 1820s, after the United States took control of Florida, another day-beacon was built. Finally, in 1826 Congress appropriated funds for the building of a major seacoast lighthouse here. The 65-foot tall masonry tower was completed and lighted on April 15, 1827. It was considered one of the finest lighthouses in the United States, but it was completely washed away in the great hurricane of October 10, 1846.

On March 3, 1847, Congress appropriated $20,000 "for a screw-pile lighthouse on or near Sand Key." In 1851, Isaiah W. P. Lewis, who had designed the Carysfort Reef Lighthouse, was chosen to design the new tower. The contract for the tower was granted to John F. Riley Ironworks in Charleston, and the lantern was to be made by J. V. Merrick and Son. Lewis oversaw the manufacture of the ironwork and the installation of the foundation pilings. Lt. George Gordon Meade had just completed the Carysfort Reef Lighthouse on March 10, 1852, and in May, he was transferred to the construction of the Sand Key Lighthouse. However, the construction funds had been expended, and it was not until September that Congress appropriated more funding. In January, 1853, work finally began.

Sand Key Lighthouse

During the spring, the iron skeleton of the unique lighthouse rose above the azure waters of the Florida Keys, and by early summer construction neared completion. Over 450 tons of iron went into the lighthouse. The dwelling for the keepers contained nine rooms, each twelve feet square. One room contained the water tanks, fed through pipes from rainwater, and storage for the lamp oil to light the lens. The enclosed stairway column which led to the lantern contained 112 steps. On the top of the lighthouse, Meade added a British-style lantern with the window astragals running diagonally. This style permitted the astragals to be narrower than vertical ones, thus allowing more light to pass through.[14] This would be the signature touch to the lighthouses that Meade worked on in Florida, and all of the lighthouses bearing this style lantern, except for the Hillsboro Inlet Lighthouse, would be ones that Meade built.

As the final stage of completion, the first Fresnel lens in Florida was installed. This huge, first-order lens had been exhibited at the 1851 Crystal Palace Exposition in London before it was shipped via New York to Florida for installation in the Sand Key Lighthouse. When the 132-foot tall lighthouse was completed, its total cost was $126,000.

Like all of the other "reef lights," the Sand Key Lighthouse experienced its share of hurricanes, the first being the devastating hurricane of 1856. The hurricane completely washed away the island and everything on it except the lighthouse. This was repeated by the hurricane of October, 1865.

Like the lighthouse at Carysfort Reef, the Sand Key Lighthouse remained in operation throughout the Civil War, but the "twin hurricanes" of October, 1870, and ones in 1874 and 1875 attacked the lighthouse. The last two hurricanes did so much damage to the keepers' quarters that they had to be rebuilt. A weather station was built on the restored island, but it was washed away in the hurricane of 1909. Rebuilt, it was demolished again by a hurricane just a year later. Another hurricane washed everything away again in 1919, but through all of this, the lighthouse stood firm.

Sand Key was noted as a bird rookery for terns and other sea birds, and their eggs were very popular with people from Key West. The bird populations were being so decimated that the American Ornithological Union formed a Bird Protection Committee. They hired people to serve as bird wardens, and the principal keeper at the Sand Key Lighthouse became one of them. However, so many people visited Sand Key that the birds finally deserted the island completely.

The Sand Key Lighthouse was automated in 1941 with an acetylene system, and the keepers were removed. With no keepers aboard, the lighthouse was subjected to much vandalism and maintenance problems which went for months without repair. The wooden floors and other wooden parts of the keepers' dwelling rotted and fell apart. Nevertheless, in 1975, the lighthouse became part of the Wilderness Preservation System and was placed on the National Register of Historic Places. In 1982, the first-order lens was removed and a modern optic took its place.

In 1989, renovation work began on the lighthouse. However, flammable materials left by the contractor somehow caught fire, and the lighthouse was seriously damaged by the conflagration. Studies proved that the structure was still serviceable, so the lighthouse was repaired for further service. Unhappily the damaged historic keepers' dwelling and stair column were completely removed. The Sand Key Lighthouse, like the other reef lights, remains in operation today.

Part 3
Lore of the Reef Lights

Lost Keepers of Sombrero Key Lighthouse

Although the United States Lighthouse Service was normally a civilian agency, during times of war, it was placed under the command of the Navy Department. The head of the nine-member Lighthouse Board was also generally a high-ranking naval officer, and, from 1884, lighthouse keepers had worn Navy-styled uniforms. When the Lighthouse Service was transferred into the United States Coast Guard in 1939, it became a full-time, official military organization, first in the Treasury Department, then the Transportation Department, and now in the Department of Homeland Security. It is appropriate, I feel, that when we remember our military servicemen, we also include those lighthouse keepers who have given their lives in the service of their duty.

Duty aboard the reef lights was not easy, and often it was dangerous, if not from storms then from the heat, humidity, insects, and diseases which then plagued this area of the world. There were deaths at many of the reef lights, but Sombrero Key Lighthouse had the most. Four men lost their lives there.

Richard White was born in England, but he had emigrated to Key West as a young man. He decided to join the United States Lighthouse Establishment and was successful in being selected to serve. On March 21, 1873, White was appointed to serve as the first assistant keeper at the Sombrero Key Lighthouse, succeeding Charles R. Johnson, who had resigned. White was paid $465 per year.

A Florida Lighthouse Keeper.

Appointed at the same time as White was Oscar Fish who would serve as second assistant keeper in place of Hiram S. Seymour who had also resigned. This was also Fish's first appointment in the lighthouse establishment. Together, these two new, raw recruits, White and Fish, arrived at the Sombrero Key Lighthouse to serve under 61-year-old Principal Keeper Adolphus A. Seymour. Seymour was born in Bermuda in July, 1811, and was a veteran of service at Sand Key and Northwest Passage. He had also served more than a year as first assistant keeper at Sombrero before being promoted to principal keeper on June 30, 1872.

Unhappily for his assistant keepers, Seymour had a personality which was so irascible that both of his previous assistant keepers resigned. Fish would remain on Sombrero only seven months, and later, two more assistants would resign due to the argumentative nature of "old man" Seymour. Through the next several months, however, White and Fish survived while Keeper Seymour trained his assistants and had them operating the Sombrero Key Lighthouse at top efficiency. One of the tasks of the keepers was to sail the small station sailboat into Key West to collect the quarterly payments for the keepers, pick up and mail letters, and also purchase supplies that the men needed. The keepers usually rotated this duty so that each man had the opportunity to learn the coastline and how to handle and sail the boat.

In late July, it was First Assistant Keeper Richard White's turn to make the trip to Key West. He successfully made the voyage down in three days. He spent another couple of days doing the errands he had to perform, and then on August 2nd, he started back to Sombrero Key Lighthouse. The trip back usually took a day or two more as it was against the normal southeast trade winds. What happened next, Keeper Seymour recorded in the light station journal:

> We saw nothing more of him [White] or the boat until August 6th at 10:00 A.M. We discovered the boat was coming from Hogg Key [at the west end of Key Vaca, since joined to it by construction fill for the Florida East Coast Railway]. It was blowing fresh and began to be getting squally. At 10:30 we saw the boat when it was struck by a squall and instantly capsized. After a few minutes the squall passed over. We saw the man floating on the collapsed boom and sail of the boat. The boat was capsized, still floating a few yards away from him. He was very visible, for at the time of the accident he was not over one and a half miles from the lighthouse. The tide set in toward us, till we could distinctly see his features and could he have assisted the spar that bore him up by swimming in the least, he would have most assuredly reached the house. The tide turned against him and swept him in a west-southwest direction about four miles from us. This was about 3:30 P.M. at which time we lost sight of him altogether. . . as soon as the boat capsized, we hoisted the ensign from the top of the tower to attract the attention of three little turtlers or spongers that were cruising about outside Knight's Key, but no one came on that day. On the following day, we hoisted the ensign again in distress to draw attention to any vessels that might pass. At 4:00 P.M. the steamer Clyde, Captain Kennedy, finally hove to and sent his boat and crew to whom I imparted the news and also delivered letters relative to the casualty to the official in Key West. The steamer happened to be one of the regular line of packets plying between New York and Galveston via Key West.

A lighthouse tender approaching the Sombrero Key Lighthouse in the late 19th century. In this photo, some of the coral heads can be seen above low water. This gave Sombrero Reef its local name of "Dry Banks." Note the American flag flying to the upper left of the keeper's dwelling. It was this ensign that was flown upside down to denote distress at the lighthouse.

First Assistant Keeper Richard White was never seen again. A week later, Major Orville B. Babcock, chief engineer for the Sixth and Seventh Lighthouse Districts arrived at Sombrero Key Lighthouse with a new boat for the two stranded keepers. With Babcock also came forty-year old William Bates to succeed White as first assistant keeper. Bates, born in England in 1832, had previously served at Dry Tortugas and Sand Key. He would later return to Sand Key as first assistant keeper and then serve for nineteen years as venerable principal keeper of the American Shoal Lighthouse, retiring on June 30, 1899.

Unfortunately for Orville Babcock, a man who had helped arrange Lee's surrender in the Civil War, he would suffer the same fate as Richard White. On June 2, 1884, while coming through the choppy waters of Mosquito (now Ponce de Leon) Inlet near Daytona Beach to begin construction of the new Mosquito Inlet

Lighthouse, the small dinghy carrying Babcock and several other men from a schooner off-shore overturned in the inlet. Babcock drowned. At least his body was recovered and returned to Washington, D.C. for burial. Richard White's body was never found.

In June, 1886, Martin Weatherford came aboard Sombrero Key Lighthouse to serve as second assistant keeper. Weatherford had been born in 1847 either in Germany or in Key West. (The records differ. Sometimes, a foreigner might claim a U.S. city as his birthplace if he thought that a U.S. birthplace might give him a better chance at a position.) Between 1880 and 1885, Weatherford had quickly come up through the ranks serving as a second and then a first assistant keeper at Alligator Reef Lighthouse. On January 2, 1885, at the age of thirty-seven, Weatherford was appointed principal keeper at the Carysfort Reef Lighthouse, for a nice annual salary of $820.

In late May or very early June of 1886, however, something happened. On June 14, 1886, Keeper Martin Weatherford suddenly found himself demoted and transferred to the position of second assistant keeper at the Sombrero Key Lighthouse. No documents yet found have explained why this happened to Martin Weatherford or what he might have done to merit the demotion.

When Weatherford arrived at the Sombrero Key Lighthouse in June, a former Navy man, Melville Evans Spencer, was the principal keeper. Spencer was born in Pennsylvania in 1851 and had served as a second and a first assistant keeper at the Jupiter Inlet Lighthouse before coming to Sombrero as principal keeper. Weatherford's immediate supervisor was the first assistant keeper, a Scotsman by the name of James Donaldson. Weatherford worked hard to redeem himself and his work was done so well that on

Sombrero Key Lighthouse. Note the lower level deck below the dwelling house.

May 7,1890, when Donaldson transferred to the Fowey Rocks Light Station, Weatherford gained his promotion to first assistant keeper at Sombrero Key.

Weatherford did his duty and served as a good first assistant keeper at the Sombrero Key Lighthouse. By 1891, he had served on the lighthouse for nearly two years. May 7th was the first anniversary of his promotion to first assistant keeper. There are no clues in the existing documents as to what happened, but on that same May 7, 1891, Keeper Spencer noted succinctly in the light station journal that First Assistant Keeper Martin Weatherford had suddenly died on Sombrero Key Lighthouse.

Michael Eickoff, a German-born man who had served on Sombrero as second assistant keeper for four months, since January 5, 1891, was promoted to Weatherford's position of first assistant keeper. In a cruel twist of fate, First Assistant Keeper Michael Eickoff himself would be the third fatality at the Sombrero Key Lighthouse.

In the late 1860s Rudolph Reike emigrated to America from Hamburg, Germany, with his wife and daughter. When their ship wrecked along the Florida reefs, the Reikes were brought to Key West by the salvors, and there the young German family decided to stay. Soon after they settled, however, Reike's wife died of smallpox, and he sent his daughter to be cared for by the nuns at the Convent of Mary Immaculate in Key West.

Perhaps due to his thick German accent or his Teutonic personality, Reike soon discovered that he did not enjoy socializing with other people. He was a loner. Reike found work in Key West not much to his liking, and he finally decided that service in the Lighthouse Establishment might be perfect for him as he could enjoy all the isolation from society he wanted out on the reef lights.

Reike's lighthouse service started in January, 1884, at the Carysfort Reef Lighthouse. He arrived as a second assistant keeper. Only nine days later, however, 26-year old first assistant keeper, William Lester, was promoted to the position of Principal Keeper of the Northwest Passage Lighthouse off Key West. Reike suddenly found himself promoted to first assistant keeper at Caryfort Reef. In August, 1893, he was appointed principal keeper of the Sombrero Key Lighthouse, succeeding Melville Evans Spencer. Reike would serve in this capacity for more than ten and a half years.

Reike enjoyed the isolation of the reef lights, and working on the ocean provided him with the mental and physical challenges that he wanted. He performed his duties as principal keeper well, but he did not socialize with the other men and seldom spoke with them or with the visitors who stopped by from passing vessels. Some of his assistants never liked him for his aloofness, although several stayed with him for several years.

Under Reike's charge at Sombrero Key Lighthouse in August, 1893, were first assistant keeper Michael Eickoff and second assistant keeper Miguel Fabal. Eickoff was a fellow German, so he and Reike immediately had something in common, although that seemed to make no difference to Reike.

Miguel Fabal was Spanish-born and had started his lighthouse service in late 1882 at the Alligator Reef Lighthouse. He had quickly worked his way up to first assistant and principal keeper at that lighthouse in only five and a half years. After serving as principal keeper for a little more than one and a half years, on the last day of 1890, he had resigned from the Lighthouse Establishment. Fabal returned to service back at the bottom as a second assistant keeper on June 10, 1892, at Sombrero Key Lighthouse.

In mid-October, 1893, Fabal had taken the station sailboat in to Key West for supplies, leaving Keeper Reike and First Assistant Keeper Michael Eickhoff to man the light. On the early morning of October 18, Keeper Reike was standing the last watch of the night in the lantern room of the tower. As the sun rose, Reike extinguished the lamp.

Usually, the assistant keeper would come up to help with hanging the lantern curtains, the cleaning of the lamp and lens, and the numerous other jobs that had to be done. With Fabal gone, Reike had expected Eickoff to come up. But he did not. Becoming curious and concerned, Reike decided to find out what was detaining First Assistant Eickoff. Reike recorded in the light station journal what he found:

"Dead the 18th [October] at 6:45 A.M. First Assistant Michael Eickhoff. I came down the stairs of the watch [room] and went down to the platform to see what he was doing and I found him dead. I set the American Ensign at once, upside down on top of the lantern tower. Weather cloudy."

Reike, to allay any suspicions of foul play, brought the assistant keeper's corpse inside the dwelling that night. Reike waited, but no ships saw his distress signal. After two days in the warmth of October, Eickoff's body had started to deteriorate, and Reike had to move it to the outside platform.

Finally, on the morning of October 21st, Captain R. Pearson of the schooner *Champion* stopped to check on the distress signal. Keeper Reike was very glad to see Captain Pearson and showed him Eickoff's body on the outside platform and explained what had happened. Pearson found Eickhoff's body badly decomposed. Pearson ferried Eickoff's body out to the *Champion*. They set sail for deeper water, and at 11:50 a.m., Eickoff was given a burial at sea.

The next and last fatality on the Sombrero Reef Lighthouse did not occur until twenty years after the Coast Guard had taken over the nation's lighthouses in 1939.

In December, 1958, twenty-one year old Seaman Willis R. Parker was assigned by the Coast Guard to serve on the Sombrero Key Lighthouse. Young Seaman Parker was born in 1937 in Homestead, Florida, and was unmarried. During his eight months on Sombrero Key Lighthouse he impressed his Coast Guard colleagues as even-tempered and self-reliant, a popular young man.

The Officer-in-Charge of the station was Boatswain's Mate First Class Furman C. Williamson. Williamson had been born in 1927 in Kannapolis, North Carolina. He joined the Navy in August, 1943, and the Coast Guard in 1947. He married and raised a family in Miami. In November, 1958, Furman was appointed to take charge of the Sombrero Key Light Station.

Parker's other comrade on the lighthouse was Seaman Donald Beckum, a native of Dade City, Florida. Beckum's wife lived in nearby Marathon, where she worked at the Marathon Sundry Store. Beckum had joined the crew at the Sombrero Reef Lighthouse in June, 1958, so he was the "old man" of the crew.

The Coast Guardsmen each served 24 days on the lighthouse and then had 6 days off. If a man wanted or needed additional time, he could deduct it from the 30 days of annual leave which the Coast Guard allowed its lighthouse personnel. The housing quarters contained two bunk rooms with cots for two men each, a head, a shower, a kitchen equipped with a four-burner butane gas stove, a stainless steel electric refrigerator, a freezer, hot water heater, weather equipment and recreational facilities consisting of two radios and a 17-inch black and white television set. Shore contact could be made through ship to shore and conventional telephones.

Despite the great location for fishing, none of the Coast Guardsmen fished, and there was not

Furman C. Williamson, Officer in Charge, when Willis Parker served aboard Sombrero Key Lighthouse.

a usable rod anywhere on the station. The only time the men had fish for dinner was when a shrimper or fishing boat dropped off a little present to the keepers. The keepers also did not enjoy swimming around their perch over one of the Keys finest coral reefs. Chief Furman apparently was scared to death of the large barracuda which swam under the lighthouse. He later told a reporter, "There is no restriction against swimming, but we just don't dare take a chance."

One afternoon in August, 1959, Seaman Parker left the lighthouse in the station launch to Marathon with a special work crew from Key West. As Beckum was then on extended leave, Station Chief Williamson was left alone on the lighthouse. Just before 7 p.m., a half hour before it would be dark and as the seas were beginning to build, Williamson saw Parker returning in the boat. Williamson went down on the lower

Seaman Donald Beckum, who also served with Parker, preparing to watch the station TV.

platform, fifteen feet above the water, to prepare to lower the block and tackle for hoisting the boat up to the platform. He lowered the heavy block and line, and Parker grabbed the block.

Just then, a large wave hit the boat and washed it away from the lighthouse. Parker should have let go of the block, but he held onto it and was lifted out of the boat. The line, with Parker hanging onto the block at its end, swung back and smacked Parker's head against one of the cast-iron pilings of the lighthouse. Parker fell into the sea. He quickly surfaced sputtering and struggling. On the platform, the horrified Williamson threw Parker a life ring. Parker grasped it and seemed to be all right. However, another wave hit him, and he lost his hold. The life ring floated away, and Parker disappeared.

Alone on the lighthouse with no boat, Williamson had no choice but to call for help on the telephone. He called the Florida Highway Patrol in Marathon and the Coast Guard headquarters in Key West. Local boats and Coast Guard cutters started out in the search. Captain

View of the bunk room which Williamson and Beckum shared at the lighthouse.

Johnny Brantner was the first to arrive on the scene in his fast boat, the *Fiesta*. It was now already dark. Brantner searched in vain for the vanished Coast Guardsman.

A Coast Guard rescue plane and helicopters arrived soon afterward, and the Coast Guard cutter *Ariadne* arrived from Key West. Charter boats from Marathon joined in the search. That night, they found the launch, drifting in the Gulf Stream about a mile from the lighthouse, but no sign of Parker.

The next day, Parker's brother came down from Homestead to join in the search, and late that afternoon, he found the body of his brother, Willis Parker. Parker's body was found laying on the bottom on Sombrero Key Reef in four feet of water, not very far from the lighthouse. There was a bump on his head apparently where he had struck the piling.

Two years before Willis Parker was killed at Sombrero Key Lighthouse, Donald Bascome served there. He took this photograph of the station boat, which could be the same one which Parker was using in his fatal accident.(Photo courtesy of Donald Bascome.)

Seaman Parker would be the last man to die on the Sombrero Key Lighthouse. In late 1960 the lighthouse was automated and keepers and Coast Guardsmen disappeared forever from the lights.

The men who served on the reef lights were hardy, dedicated men. Some of them lost their lives in the line of duty. It is appropriate that we remember them. Perhaps someday, a memorial in view of the Sombrero Key Lighthouse, perhaps on Sombrero Beach, could be erected in their honor.

Editor's note: Tom Taylor was a resident of Marathon, Key Vaca, the nearest land to the Sombrero Key Light.

G.S.

Stormy Weather on the Reef Lights

The word "hurricane" comes from the Spanish word huracan, which was itself derived from the language of the West Indies Arawak Indians. Apparently, it meant "storm." Christopher Columbus sailed on his first voyage of discovery during the hurricane season, but he was very lucky. He did not experience his first hurricane until his second voyage when he was off the Isle of Pines of the south shore of Cuba. The Spanish later lost two treasure fleets in the hurricanes of 1622 and 1733 in the Keys. The famous *Atocha* sank in that first storm. Ships from the latter storm still lie in the waters of the Keys as well.

It is appropriate to look at some of the other storms which hit the reef lights and honor the men who stayed at their posts and weathered these blows from nature.

In February, 1881, Kentucky-born L. C. Warner had just received a promotion from second assistant keeper to first assistant keeper at the Carysfort Reef Lighthouse. Captain Edward Bell was the principal keeper. No new second assistant keeper had yet been appointed. From the first extant lighthouse journal for the Carysfort Reef Lighthouse, we learn from the February 4th entry that a storm is brewing. Captain Bell writes: "The wind is east by south and very scully, the barometer 29.74."

Minots Ledge Lighthouse collapsing in an 1850 hurricane.

During the night, the sea becomes rough, breaking heavily on the nearby reef, and for the next several days, the wind continues "to blow a very fresh breeze." Fortunately, this was a relatively mild storm and just one of dozens which the Carysfort Reef Lighthouse has gone through.

When George W. Parsons visited the lighthouse in 1875, he noted a motto, "God with Us," inscribed on the pedestal of the lens near the revolving mechanism platform. When he asked Keeper Bell about this, Bell replied: "Indeed we need Him badly enough out here sometimes...when the hurricane comes down on us and this whole thing [the lighthouse] totters and shakes as though it were about to fall."

It could be a harrowing experience for the keepers out on those sea-swept lighthouses. Although the reef lights have proved themselves through the "test of time," most keepers on these lighthouses probably knew about the ill-fated iron-pile Minot's Ledge Lighthouse off Massachusetts which collapsed in a storm in 1850 with the loss of two keepers.

Storms often brought with them shipwrecks near the lighthouses. On June 17, 1874, Keeper George Richard Billberry, Sr., at the Alligator Reef Lighthouse, reported that in a squall an English vessel, loaded with lumber, had grounded on a nearby reef. A month later, when "the wind was strong, many squalls . . .," an American bark with a load of sugar bound to New York grounded near the lighthouse. The wreckers were able to save her. Billberry noted a September storm: "Blowing a gale all night, heavy rain squalls, sea running very high and breaking heavy around this station . . . three masted schooner *Florence Rodgers* from Jamaica for New York loaded with logwood, on shore close by Indian Key. She lost topmast and nearly all sails during gale."

John W. Frow was the first keeper of the Fowey Rocks Lighthouse when it went into operation on June 15, 1878. Only three months later, Frow and his assistants went through their first storm on the new lighthouse. The winds reached more than 100 miles per hour. Frow recorded in the station journal for September 6, that as the winds increased, the keepers secured the lighthouse boat to an upper platform of the tower. Just after midnight, "there was a heavy hurricane blowing and increasing rapidly. The glass of the lantern leaked badly." For the next twenty-four hours, the keepers at Fowey Rocks worked to keep things dry, mopping the lantern floor, wiping down the lens, and keeping the light burning in the midst of the black gale. Frow wrote: "Eastern door of dwelling [is] so strained one of the panels is almost off and starting to tear the other off."

For three days the hurricane raged. The lantern windows were working loose from their putty, "allowing the rain into the lantern constantly." Finally, on September 11, the barometer began to rise.

Damaged weather station with Sand Key Lighthouse in the background.

"The gale broke and the wind came around to the southwest," Keeper Frow wrote with relief. The Fowey Rocks Lighthouse had survived its first hurricane.

In 1909 and twice in 1910, the Sand Key Lighthouse went through some terrible hurricanes. At that time, a United States Weather Bureau station was located near the lighthouse on the tiny sand islet. C. J. Doherty was the weather station keeper. The journals for the light station itself are no longer extant, but Doherty's log does survive, and Doherty, through this journal, gives us an idea of these hurricanes at Sand Key. Doherty was not at the station during the hurricane of October 11, 1909, when the winds gusted up to a hundred miles per hour. The weather station keeper returned to his station the day after the hurricane. The *Key West Journal* for October 13, 1909, reported:

> Weather observer Doherty returned last night from Sand Key where he went to examine the damages sustained by the weather station there. He states everything on Sand Key was blown completely away, except the lighthouse, and that was damaged to some extent. No lives were lost . . . as every person there repaired to the lighthouse during the first part of the storm. The barometer fell to 28.32

inches, 14 points lower than at Key West. The sea overran Sand Key twenty feet high, coming to the top flight of steps on the lighthouse. Several windows were blown out, and the draft was so strong that the combined strength of several men could not open the doors below.

The keepers on duty at the Sand Key Lighthouse at this time were Principal Keeper Charles G. Johnson, First Assistant Keeper Theophilus Sawyer, and Second Assistant Keeper Richard Palmer (who had just reported to duty from American Shoal the month before).

The following October, 1910, the infamous "twin" hurricanes hit Sand Key. The second was the worst with 125 mph winds with winds above gale force for more than thirty hours. Doherty, who this time had taken refuge with the keepers in the lighthouse, later reported:

This station was visited by two severe hurricanes on October 13th, 14th, and 15th, and October 17th and 18th. The wind velocity steadily increased and much rain fell . . .Waves began to wash over the island, and soon all the sand was carried away from under the lighthouse, and the island shifted to a position further north...An outhouse was washed away . . . at noon on the 17th the wharf and woodpile were washed away, and the lighthouse began to sway in the gusts. Great trouble was experienced in keeping the doors closed on the windward side, the force of the wind pulling out nails repeatedly . . . rain fell in torrents, making it impossible to see further than 100 feet...The wind velocity increased and the swaying and trembling of the lighthouse stopped the clock several times. . . the boathouse went to pieces and was washed to sea. At. 1:30 p.m. the brick oil house broke up. At 1:50 p.m... the barometer reached its lowest point, 28.40 inches...braces at the bottom of the lighthouse began to break, and the force of the waves kept striking them against the other iron like sledgehammers.

Charles G. Johnson was still principal keeper of the Sand Key Lighthouse during the 1910 hurricanes. William A. Albury was First Assistant Keeper, and Stanley Saunders was Second Assistant Keeper.

The Labor Day Hurricane of 1935 ran directly over Alligator Reef Light. It is amazing that any structure could survive 200 mph winds -- but Alligator did. Assistant Keeper James Duncan said later that a rogue wave engulfed the lower platform. "How I held on and why I wasn't drowned, I can't say."

One of the strongest of the storms of the last half of the twentieth century was a category four storm known as Hurricane Donna, and it hit hardest at the Sombrero Key Lighthouse. The entire lower platform of the lighthouse was ripped off. Fortunately, the living quarters, forty feet above normal sea level, survived without major damage. Throughout the storm, the men kept the light burning. The Coast Guardsmen assigned to the Sombrero Key Lighthouse in 1960 were Boatswain Mate First Class Furman C. Williamson, Engineman Ernest Bryan, Seaman Cecil Bryan, and Seaman Donald Beckman.

The Adventures of Keeper Benjamin Howard Lowe, Sr.

Benjamin Howard Lowe until recently was not included in any published lists of Keys lighthouse keepers. This man, however, served at four Florida lighthouses, including two of the reef lights and at Dry Tortugas and Sanibel Island. This is his and his family's story.

The ancestry and background of Benjamin Howard Lowe, Sr., is similar to that of many of the other keepers who served on the reef lights. His father, Captain Arthur Alese Lowe, Sr., was born on August 6, 1866, on Green Turtle Key in the Abaco Islands of the Bahamas. He was the son of Jabez Lowe, from a family which had emigrated to Green Turtle Key from England in the early 1800s, and Amelia A. Curry. Arthur Lowe grew up with the sea as a sailor and fisherman. When he was 20, he married a local girl, Jane Euphemia Lowe, also in the Curry family, and emigrated to the Keys in 1886 or 1887, when he worked for William Curry & Sons as a seaman and a wrecker. He became a naturalized U. S. citizen on September 18, 1893. For eight years, he captained the 44-ton, two-masted schooner *Magnolia*, carrying freight and passengers between Key West and Miami. Arthur Lowe may have commanded this vessel when it laid the submarine telephone cable between the United States and Cuba. In 1919, the schooner was swept out to sea by a hurricane and lost, but Captain Lowe was not then on board. He had settled in Key West, where he had four daughters and two sons. One son died in infancy, but the surviving son was Benjamin Howard Lowe, Sr., born on August 30, 1898.

American Shoal Lighthouse

Benjamin Howard Lowe, Sr., preferred to be called "Howard." Young Howard took to the sea as had his father, serving on the *Magnolia* with his father. Later he served as a cook on sponge boats and as a sailor and mate on a large number of vessels, mostly two-masted schooners. Howard's first wife died suddenly without children, and in 1921 he married Mary Caridad Alvarez, by whom he would have three children in Key West: Mary Louise, Benjamin Howard, Jr., and Roy Elwood. In the 1920s Howard, Mary and his father farmed key limes and vegetables on Key Largo or Elliot Key, leaving baby Mary Louise in Key West in care of relatives. In 1929, to provide a more stable income for his family, Howard Lowe joined the United States Lighthouse Service as an assistant keeper. Lowe was assigned to the Fowey Rocks Lighthouse, off Miami, the furthest reef light from Key West. To keep his family closer to him, Howard moved them to Coconut Grove. At the Fowey Rocks Light Station, First Assistant Keeper Lowe served with Principal Keeper Richard Palmer and Second Assistant Keeper Hamilton S. Perry. In the top of the tower, Lowe would spend many days cleaning and polishing the huge first-order Fresnel lens. In 1923, the Fowey Rocks Lighthouse had gotten its own telephone, and in 1929, Keeper Lowe could use this to keep in touch with his family ashore. The keepers also had a crystal radio set and could enjoy radio concerts from Philadelphia, Boston, and New York! In 1930, Howard's wife Mary gave birth to their fourth and last child, daughter Julia Camille. During the difficult birth, Mary began to hemorrhage, and Keeper Howard had to give blood for the transfusions. Mary would never again enjoy good health.

Perhaps because of this difficult birth and his wife's ill health, Lowe decided to move the family back to Key West where he had a support network. He applied for and got the position of assistant keeper at the Dry Tortugas Lighthouse on Loggerhead Key. Lowe served under Principal Keeper Andrew Albury. Osmund McKinney, who would soon leave for Sanibel Island, was serving as Second Assistant Keeper during 1928-1932. Later, "Pip" Pippen served as Second Assistant Keeper. Antonio Canalejo, who married Howard Lowe's younger sister Edna Genieva, served a stint as an assistant keeper, and Stanley Franklin "Mickey" Saunders, the brother-in-law married to Howard's older sister Lillie Mayfield, also served at the Dry Tortugas.

Here at Loggerhead Key, Lowe could spend more time with his family, spending winter leave time in Key West with them. During the summer months, when school was out, the entire family would voyage out to the Dry Tortugas to spend the summer with their father at the light station, living on the second floor of the station's duplex dwelling. Howard's youngest son, Roy, remembers that the Carnegie Institute had a laboratory on the north end of the island where scientists were doing experiments with shark livers. Young Roy loved to fish and gladly caught sharks for the scientists who paid

Dry Tortugas Lighthouse

him 25 cents per shark. Their research paid off as they discovered in the sharks' livers a lubricating substance which would ease the strain and dryness of the eyes of fighter pilots during World War II. In the mid-1930's however, young Roy Lowe was more interested in the pies and other delicacies the scientists' cook shared with him.

Roy's love of fishing once got him into a bit of trouble. He had often gone out fishing with his father in the station motor boat. One day, little Roy decided to go out by himself. He got the motor started fine and headed out. However, he did not know how to turn the engine off, and he motored around until the engine ran out of gas. Then, Roy anchored and fished. As the sun was setting and he couldn't get the motor started again for his return trip home, Roy knew he was in trouble. In the meantime, his father had spied him out at sea from the top of the lighthouse tower. With no other boat on shore to use to go and rescue his son, Keeper Howard Lowe swam out to a larger lighthouse boat which was anchored

Keeper Benjamin Howard Lowe, Sr. and his second wife, Mary Caridad Alvarez, taken in Key West in the 1930s. (Photo by Gloria Saladino)

about 200 yards offshore. Then he went after young Roy. The young fisherman had a warm bottom that night!

Sometimes, things could get spooky on the remote island. One night, as Roy sat near a huge rubber tree, a "ghost" suddenly appeared and scared the 6-year-old boy out of his wits. But it was only Uncle Mickey Saunders, walking under and carrying a small step-ladder with a sheet thrown over it! That rubber tree was a favorite with Roy, and it was usually filled with birds, but Roy remembers when a hurricane came through, and the next morning there were thousands of dead birds under that rubber tree. During the hurricane, the families forsook the dwellings and sought refuge in the sturdy brick tower.

"The Lighthouse Kids": Benjamin H., Jr., Mary Louise, Roy E. Sr., and Julia Lowe.(Photo by Gloria Saladino)

The station's boat house was not one of little Roy's favorite places. Howard Lowe was a very religious man, and he set a strict policy for the observance of the Sabbath for his family. On Sunday, there was no ball playing and no singing, unless it was the singing of hymns. The family would gather to listen to church services on the station's radio set. After a large Sunday dinner, Keeper Lowe would lead his family to the boat house where a one hour laying-down "siesta" was enforced. Being at the boathouse was a terrible temptation for little Roy. The boy could hardly restrain himself with the sights of all those fish to catch nearby. He could not rest; he wanted to get up and go out fishing!

The children at the light station always loved it when a Mr. Krippendorff from Pennsylvania would visit. He always brought down boxes of candy for the children, and he loved to fish almost as much as young Roy. One day, Keeper Lowe took Krippendorff and young Roy out fishing in the station launch. Looking down into the crystal clear water from the bow of the boat, young Roy spotted what he thought was a ten pound grouper on the bottom right below the boat. He called to his dad to come over for a look. For a while, Keeper Lowe was reluctant, but at the continued insistence of his son, he finally came over for a look. Little Roy was astonished when his father suddenly dashed below the deck of the launch and came up with a stout rope with a huge hook on the end. Lowe attached a yellowtail snapper to the hook and threw it over. In a moment, there was a tug on the line. Lowe and Mr. Krippendorff struggled to land the "ten-pound grouper." When they got it aboard, Roy learned it was a 502-pound jewfish! The lighthouse keeper decided to donate the fish to the hungry crew of the visiting lighthouse tender *Ivy*, who that day had caught a 100-pound barracuda for supper. They were delighted to scrap their plans for tough barracuda steak in favor of delicious jewfish. The huge barracuda was unceremoniously dropped overboard.

Not every visit out to the Dry Tortugas Light Station was joyous for the Lowe family. One summer, the entire family became very ill from food poisoning, and a Navy doctor was sent from Key West by seaplane to attend to the family. It is believed that an opened and improperly stored can of corned beef was the culprit. Another medical emergency occurred one summer during the family's annual visit when young Julia had to be transported back to Key West for stitches. She tried to throw an ax up into a coconut tree to bring down a coconut as she had seen the men do on several occasions. Unfortunately, the ax blade landed on her foot, and she bears the scar from the failed attempt.

At the Dry Tortugas Light Station, Assistant Keeper Lowe helped with the operation of the radio beacon which had been installed in 1926. The signal was relayed through a structural steel tower near the lighthouse. The old oil storage house of the lighthouse had been converted into the home for the electronics for the beacon, and the house had been attached to the lighthouse by a concrete passageway. In 1931, the radio beacon generators were connected to a powerful electric lamp in the lantern, and its three million candlepower beam became at that time the most powerful light in the United States, about 250 times brighter than the old oil lamps it replaced. Undoubtedly, Lowe was relieved by the easier operation which the electric lamp afforded the keepers over its oil-fueled predecessor.

Lowe was probably stationed at the Dry Tortugas when the Great Labor Day Hurricane struck Islamorada in 1935. Happily, at Dry Tortugas, Lowe would have missed the worst part of this storm, and there was no major damage at this station.

Not too long after the hurricane, Lowe transferred to another reef light - the American Shoal Lighthouse where he was even closer to his family at Key West. However, the family made few visits out to this light station. On one rare visit, son Roy remembers having to cross a gangplank from the boat to the landing platform. As Roy began to cross the narrow plank, his father called out to him to be careful and pointed out a school of thousands of barracudas in the water below. Roy was scared to death of barracudas. The boy became so nervous that he lost his footing and fell in. He thought he was a goner, but the barracudas were more afraid of him than he was of them, and they scattered in a heartbeat. After that, Roy Lowe lost his fear of barracudas.

These experiences were good for Howard Lowe's son, however, Roy was now getting to that difficult adolescent stage where he was skipping school and getting into considerable trouble at home in Key West. The boy's mother was chronically ill, and his older sister was an invalid. Roy needed the closer supervision of his father. Thus, by 1939, at about the time the lighthouses were transferred to the care of the United States Coast Guard, Howard Lowe had transferred to the Sanibel Island Lighthouse where his family could live with him all the time at this land-based light station.

The Lowe family with their two sons and two daughters arrived at the Sanibel Island Light Station with their possessions and car aboard the lighthouse tender *Ivy*, and they moved into the keeper's dwelling on the east side of the lighthouse. Here, Assistant Keeper Lowe opted to join the Coast Guard as a serviceman rather than remain as a civilian keeper. Richard Palmer, under whom Lowe had served at Fowey Rocks ten years before, was

Sanibel Island Lighthouse

now Principal Keeper at Sanibel Island. Roy remembers that the former Principal Keeper, Clarence Rutledge, who had served since 1920, had retired before 1939 but continued to live on the island. The keepers at Sanibel had the additional work of tending a large number of navigational buoy lights up and down the coast in Charlotte Harbor and San Carlos Bay. This could be dangerous work from small boats, and Roy often worried that his father might not come home some night.

When World War II broke out 17-year-old Benjamin Howard Lowe, Jr. joined the Coast Guard, leaving two hands less to help with the work around the station. However, the family pitched in to take up the slack. They soon got interested in collecting sea shells which they discovered they could sell to the shell factories for extra income. This would be a business they continued for many years afterwards.

In 1943 Howard Lowe suffered a double tragedy. In June his father died, and then, on Christmas Eve, his wife Mary, who had been ill for years, died of cancer at a Fort Myers hospital. The distraught assistant lighthouse keeper began suffering heart problems. Because of this, in July, 1944, Keeper Benjamin Howard Lowe, Sr. resigned from the Coast Guard after fifteen years of service as a lighthouse keeper. He moved the family once again to Key West.

In his later years, Lowe lived in Miami where he operated a shell factory and business with his son Howard Jr.. Often, they would return to Sanibel to collect shells together. Howard married twice more while he lived in the Miami area. Despite years of complaining about aches and ailments, former assistant keeper of Florida lighthouses, Benjamin Howard Lowe, Sr., outlived three of his four wives and died on March 8, 1989, in his 91st year.

Son Roy's love of fishing turned into a 45-year career as Capt. Roy E. Lowe, the Native Guide fishing from the Bahia Honda basin. In February, 1953, Captain Roy Elwood Lowe, Sr. moved his family from a 12'x12' "home" on the east end of Bahia Honda Key to a new homestead he constructed on Vaca Road (now named 50th Street, Gulf). Roy lived there with his wife, Elizabeth "Bess" Ratering Lowe, and their children, Nancy, Betty, Toni, and Roy, Jr. (Bess lived at the residence until 1992.) The Lowe children grew up in Marathon, later moving away but returning each Thanksgiving holiday to renew their roots in the Middle Keys city.

Many thanks for the information in this article are due to Roy E. Lowe, Sr., who recorded his memories in a videotape made September, 2001 by Hib Casselberry of the Florida Lighthouse Association, and to Roy's daughter Betty Lowe Phelps who queried many relatives in her research into her grandfather's lighthouse service. Betty relied on information provided by Julia Lowe Smith and Alfred Allen Lowe along with the genealogy compiled by Rachael Day Lowe to piece together B. H. Lowe's life story.

The Ghost of the Carysfort Reef Lighthouse

There are most likely many ghosts at the unique off-shore iron towers, but the "Ghost of the Carysfort Reef Lighthouse" has been a famous one.

For many years the keepers and various visitors at the Carysfort Reef Lighthouse were startled by sudden, strange groaning noises at night in the old iron lighthouse. To many, these sounds could only be those made by a ghost. The mystery of who this ghost was puzzled many people. During a visit and overnight at the lighthouse, however, a man by the name of Charles M. Brookfield may have preserved for posterity the identity of the elusive but very prominent ghost.

Charles M. Brookfield moved from Philadelphia in 1925 to build and live in a house on Elliott Key, south of the Miami area. Through the years, he was fascinated by this tropical area and its history, and he contributed many articles to local and statewide historical journals.

One of his favorite places to visit was the Carysfort Reef Lighthouse. Many times he stopped by in his boat, the *Manatee*, to deliver "goodies" to the keepers there. He was fascinated by the ghost story that he heard and encouraged the keepers to someday let him spend the night at the lighthouse to check out the story. When he got his chance, Brookfield attempted to develop a scientific rationalization for the origin of the groaning in the lighthouse. But was he right? Or is there really a ghost at the Carysfort Reef Lighthouse? In the work below, excerpted from "Mystery at Carysfort," an article he wrote in 1980, Brookfield tells of his visit to the Carysfort Reef Lighthouse in 1927 and of the ghost who lurked therein.

The 112-foot-high lighthouse built on the reef was lighted in 1852. It replaced the lightship formerly anchored inside the reef but frequently blown off station. Carysfort is the oldest of the great reef lights. Solid iron piles support it. From the lower platform, 10 feet above the sea, an iron stairway leads up to the lower floor of the two-story dwelling, 20 feet above the lower platform.

The dwelling is built of heavy sheet iron. From the center of the dwelling an iron, enclosed winding stairway leads up over 80 feet to the beacon 100 feet above the sea. The top of the dwelling serves to collect rainwater, which drains down into a big circular tank in the center of the lower floor. From an approaching boat it resembles a huge canned plum pudding with a flat top and slightly sloping sides.

Two open galleries with iron railings encircle the lighthouse, one at the lower floor and the other far above the sea at the small glass-enclosed chamber surrounding the beacon itself.

[On this visit in 1927,] the delighted keepers greeted us with cheers of 'Here comes Santa Claus.' They were Captain Jenks and his first assistant Harry Baldwin, both from Key West. The Captain was hospitality itself and Harry all smiles. They invited us to stay on and enjoy some of the food we had brought. We gladly accepted.

There were five of us for dinner: the keepers, my two friends Earl Montgomery and young Louis Murray, and myself. Harry

Carysfort Reef Lighthouse in 1927.

was the cook. Preparing the meal required lighting all three burners on the kerosene stove and I noticed that Harry used only one match to light the first burner, quickly blowing out the match and putting the burnt matchstick aside. Then, as the other burners were needed, he lighted the matchstick from the first burner and used it to light each of the other burners in turn. This action brought home to me how frugal these men must be in order to subsist and provide for their own families on the mainland on the small salary the U. S. Lighthouse Service paid.

Dinner over, we prepared to depart before the regulation time, whereon Captain Jenks asked:

"Aren't you having engine trouble?"

I told him I didn't think so, but he insisted that I start up the *Manatee* anyway. He followed me to the lower platform and waited while I boarded the boat and started the engine.

The engine ran smoothly. He called down:

"It's missing and you are in distress."

I came back up the platform ready to argue the point with him when he said, "Yes, in distress and you will have to spend the night."

Slowly it dawned on me that the regulation requiring us to leave ended with the words, "except in cases of distress."

After it was decided we should spend the night, the captain expressed his pleasure by singing a verse from "I'm Captain Jinks (Jenks) of the Horse Marines."

There was only one vacant bed available, belonging to second assistant Hall who was on 'honeymoon,' what we would call shore leave. I was offered the bed but declined and the crew of the *Manatee* took the mattresses off the boat and spread them on the floor around the big cistern. That done, we climbed the winding stairway to watch the keepers light the lamp.

The big Fresnel magnifying lens, higher than my head, was mounted on a pedestal in the middle of the small glass-enclosed room, surrounded on the outside by the upper gallery. First the keepers removed the curtains hanging inside the room that protected the lens from the rays of the sun which was just about to set. Tentatively, I pushed the lens lightly with one finger and was amazed to find that even such a slight pressure made it revolve on its smooth bearings.

Then I watched as the kerosene fuel was preheated in a tube to provide the gas for the mantle. While this was going on I stepped out onto the gallery to enjoy a magnificent view of the reef with its huge coral heads and purple sea fans waving as the gentle sea broke and washed over the reef, so shallow that at low tide many of the rocks were exposed.

Coming back into the room, I was in time to see the clock weights being wound up from down in the tower to provide the power to turn the lens. It took 45 minutes for them to run down whereupon a bell warned the keepers to wind them up again. The lamp was gleaming and turning on its pedestal. Three flashes and a blank in succession, identifying Carysfort Reef to passing mariners. Fowey Rocks, 40 miles to the north, flashed twice. Hanging outside the outer plain glass of the room were the red glass screens, exactly arranged to provide the red sectors that changed the light from white to red to warn vessels when they came too close to the reef.

Captain Jenks sat in his chair by the door opening onto the gallery, starting the first watch. The rest of us descended the winding stairway to the dwelling.

Harry Baldwin tried to put a call through to his family in Key West on the telephone that had recently been installed with a long cable that lay along the reef for six miles, connecting with the lines on Key Largo. He told me that Congresswoman Ruth Bryan Owen had secured the appropriation for its installation. There must have been trouble on the line for after repeated crankings on the handle on the wall box phone there was no response. Harry then went to get some sleep as he was to take the second watch.

Manatee's crew went to the lower floor to stretch out after a long and interesting day. I relaxed and it seemed that I had hardly closed my eyes when a loud groan shook the room and startled me awake. I sat up thinking it may have been a dream. Then another groan came and I knew it was real. I said:

"Earl, did you hear that?" His only response was a soft snore.

"Lou, did you hear anything?"

"Huh? What?" he answered sleepily.

I grabbed my flashlight and went up to the second floor. By the sound of the heavy breathing coming from Harry's door I knew that he was asleep. But there was no sleep for me.

I climbed the stairway around and around to the beacon where the captain sat reading, the cool night air coming in through the open door while the big lens slowly revolved. After some trivial conversation, I finally got around to what was on my mind.

"Captain, have you ever heard strange noises on this light?"

Captain Alexander C. Jenks, principal Keeper, and first assistant keeper, Harry Baldwin, in 1927 when Brookfield visited the lighthouse.

"Oh, yes, he replied. 'That's old Captain Johnson. You know, he died aboard this light, and he still comes around at night and groans. He must have been a great sinner. Sometimes he rattles his chains."

Captain Jenks seemed not in the least disturbed by these revelations. Just old stuff to him, but they were not reassuring for me. However, there was nothing to do but to go below and make the best of it.

Sleep would not come and after some time, I again climbed the tower. The watch had changed and Harry was winding up the clock weights in response to the warning bell I had heard on the way up the stairs.

After a few words of greeting, I went out on the gallery. The words of Joseph Conrad came to me: "A quiet night, thick with stars above, rather dark on the water."

I could see the running lights of two approaching vessels. I told Harry about how pleasant it must be to hear music from passing cruise ships, stalling before asking the question still on my mind.

"Yes it is," said Harry. "One night I heard music. It played 'Home, Sweet Home' all the way through, but when I went out on the gallery there was no ship in sight."
I never asked my question. I returned below to my cot. Pondering the events of the night, an explanation for the groans came to me. During the day, the hot sun gradually expanded the iron of the dwelling, and the cool night air caused the iron to contract rather rapidly producing the groaning sounds, startlingly human. My theory may not be true but I have clung to it ever since. But why did old Captain Johnson rattle his chains? Now there is no one there to hear him. Carysfort light is now fully automated.

That is Charles Brookfield's account of his encounter with the "Ghost of Carysfort Reef Lighthouse" and his explanation for the unearthly noises he heard. The keepers at the lighthouse apparently referred to the ghost as being that of a "Captain Johnson," a former keeper.

Well, Keeper Charles M. Johnson turns out to have been a real person. Unhappily, we know very little about this early Florida Keys keeper as most of the early records of the United States Lighthouse Establishment/Service were lost in a Commerce Department Building fire in Washington, D.C., in 1921. However, according to the scant records that we do have, we learn that Charles M. Johnson was first appointed captain of the Carysfort Reef Lightship *Florida* on October 22, 1846.[15]

When the new Caryfort Reef Lighthouse was completed in 1852, the lightship captain was appointed the first principal keeper of the new lighthouse at an annual salary of $700. Thus, Keeper Charles M. Johnson first lighted the lamps in the Carysfort Reef Lighthouse on March 10, 1852. Keeper Johnson must have greatly appreciated the more stable and roomy accommodations of the lighthouse over the rolling and more tempestuous life aboard the old lightship.

Apparently, Keeper Johnson was well regarded. On July 31, 1852, in a letter to the Lighthouse Board, Lt. George Gordon Meade, the man who had completed the building of the lighthouse, commended the new keepers as "Intelligent and faithful persons." He continued that "attention on the part of the keepers is in reality more efficient than under conditions it would be."

According to the records, however, Keeper Johnson enjoyed his service on the Carysfort Reef Lighthouse apparently for only about six months. On September 15, 1852, he was succeeded as keeper by Courtland P. Williams. Williams transferred to Carysfort Reef from Sand Key where he had been keeper since November 19, 1850. Nothing in the records shed any further light on what happened to the mysterious Charles M. Johnson. We do not know where or when he was born or any of his other duties with the Lighthouse Establishment except for on the lightship and lighthouse at Carysfort Reef. His career seems to have ended at Carysfort Reef. Is it possible that the keepers' tradition that the ghost is his indicates that he died on the lighthouse, perhaps in early September, 1852? If so, does his ghost still inhabit the old lighthouse?

Whether the ghost of Keeper Charles M. Johnson truly still inhabits the lighthouse or not, the ghostly noises continue. The only problem today is that no one hears this ghost anymore as the lighthouse is automated. Today, the ghost of Charles M. Johnson rattles his chains only for the silence of a deserted lighthouse and any other ghosts which might be there.

Ed Note: Brookfield's article was printed in Update, *May 1980. Used with permission of the Historical Museum of Southern Florida.*

The Keepers Frow:
The Adventures of Simon Frow

Simon Frau was a man whose life was guided by shipwrecks and yet whose profession was preventing them. He was born on January 22, 1808, in Mahon on the Spanish Island of Menorca in the Mediterranean. Simon was the son of Juan Frau and Margarita Pons. With the completion of the boy's formal education in 1824, the 16-year-old lad decided to delay further education and sail to distant ports around the world. Simon's family was wealthy and had a fleet of merchant ships. Leaving an explanatory letter to his mother, widowed three years earlier, Simon stole away on one of the family's ships for a seven-year voyage. The boy remained hidden in the bowels of the ship for several days, eating food he had stashed aboard, until the vessel had passed Gibraltar and entered the choppy Atlantic Ocean. Simon knew that the vessel was now too far at sea for it to return him home.

With little else to do, the captain made Simon a part of the crew, and the boy would work his way around the world. The ship stopped at Madeira, Cape Town, Madagascar, and, India on its voyage. In Singapore, the vessel was refurbished after its two-year voyage. She would now retrace her steps westward to meet a sister ship in the Azores before heading west across the Atlantic to America. Crossing the Indian Ocean on this return voyage, young Simon learned the arts of navigation. The ship did rendezvous with its sister ship in the Azores, and Simon was able to send to his mother a stack of letters he had written during the voyage. He could have gone aboard the other vessel and returned home, but he decided to stay with his ship and sail to America.

After a stormy but safe voyage, the ship arrived in Havana, Cuba. The vessel had been only a few hours out of Havana bound for its next port when a strong gale caught her and held her in its grip for three days, dragging the vessel off course. Approaching the shallow waters of the Florida Keys, the vessel was able to anchor to prevent shipwreck. However, some major damage had been done to the spars and rigging, and the seams were leaking. She would need a major refitting. The nearest port was Key West, so the captain put in there. Young Simon quickly found Key West to be a place of his liking, and he decided to stay.

The captain paid off Simon for his services and even gave him a bonus. Simon gave the captain a long letter to deliver to Simon's mother, and the captain said he would make Key West a regular port of call for his ship to check on Simon and bring him news of his family.

The captain kept his word, and on his next voyage to Key West, he even brought along Simon's younger brother, Joseph, who had wished to follow in Simon's path. Simon Frau became a naturalized American citizen on August 24, 1836. Teenaged Joseph lived with his brother and was naturalized on November 5, 1839.

 Simon's mother continually begged her son to return home and run the family business. With some pangs of guilt, Simon finally embarked on a ship to Menorca. The ship was wrecked. Simon was rescued and returned to Key West. On two other occasions, the wayward son tried to return home, and twice more, his ship was wrecked. On the last shipwreck, in sight of some islands, the crew tried to swim ashore. Simon, because he could not swim, however, elected to remain on the overturned hull of the wrecked ship. Fortune smiled on Simon this time, as the other men perished, and Simon was rescued by a passing ship the next day. With three shipwrecks under his belt, Simon decided the fates were against him in returning to Menorca, and he never tried again. In later years, when his mother begged him to send over one of his sons, Simon refused, fearing the curse might also descend on his progeny.

On October 30, 1839, Simon Frau married Sarah Ann Thrift in Key West. Sarah Ann had been born in the Bahamas, as had been so many of the other early settlers of Key West. In some legal documents of the time, Simon's name was misread and rewritten as "Frow." Simon never corrected the error, and the new spelling of the name has stuck. In many documents, also, his first name has been spelled "Simeon," although his descendants adamantly insist that he always referred to himself as and was known to the family as "Simon" Frow. (In his resignation letter in 1880, he signs his name as "Simmon" Frow.)

In September, 1847, Simon Frow purchased from William Adelaide a lot at 412 Caroline Street in Key West. He built a home, and here all but the first two of his six children would be born–three sons followed by three daughters.

In Key West, Simon worked as a pilot and wrecker. He worked for the firm of William Curry and was master of the wrecking schooner *Florida*, one of the fastest vessels of her day. Captain Frow had the opportunity to prove this one day when he outdistanced a pirate vessel which was intent on capturing the *Florida*. Because of the *Florida's* great speed, Simon Frow's wrecking vessel was often the first one to the scene of a wreck, making Frow "wreck-master" and the principal salvor of the wreck. In the records of the wrecking court in Key West his name can be found in many of the cases.

In the late summer of 1855, Charles S. Barron resigned as keeper of the Cape Florida Lighthouse, near what is today the City of Miami. The Lighthouse Board in Washington asked the Collector of Customs and Superintendent of Lights in Key West to recommend a successor. Mr. P. Baldwin replied to Washington: "I have the honor to nominate for the Principal Keeper of the Light House at Cape Florida, in lieu of Chas. S. Baron, resigned, Simeon Frow. Capt. Frow is an old shipmaster and is fully competent to discharge the duties as Light Keeper and has been a resident of this Coast for the past thirty years." Simon Frow got the job and was officially appointed on September 14, 1859.

A sketch of Cape Florida Lighthouse in 1851.

As Frow and his family rowed towards the landing on the south end of Key Biscayne, the new keeper must have wondered if he was doing the right thing for his family. His children had grown up in the comfort and relative civilization of Key West. Now they would be living in a virtual wilderness. Twenty-three years before, the Seminole Indians had attacked the lighthouse and killed and wounded its keepers. In that attack in 1836, the Indians had burned out the wooden stairway of the lighthouse, and the light had remained dark throughout the war. It was not until 1846 that a new tower had replaced the damaged one. Now, in 1859, the Third Seminole War had only recently ended, and there were still plenty of Indians about.

Four keepers had preceded the fifty-two year old Simon Frow as keeper of this second lighthouse. It took a special breed of man...and wife, to survive in this wilderness. Did the Frow family have what it took to stand the test of survival here? With Simon Frow when he arrived at the Cape Florida Lighthouse in September 1859, were his thirty-nine year old, Bahamian-born wife, Sarah Ann, nineteen-year old son John W., ten-year-old son Joseph T., and one-year-old daughter Sarah. John R. Paynor, who was already serving as assistant keeper at the lighthouse, would continue to serve until late 1861.

In 1861, when the Civil War broke out, the Confederate Secretary of the Navy, Stephen Mallory, who had lived in Key West, ordered the lighthouses put out of business so as not to aid the Federal blockading fleet. A small group of Confederate sympathizers ransacked lighthouses around Florida, carrying out this order. At Cape Florida, keepers Simon Frow and John Paynor soon met their own "band of lawless persons." That band of Confederate sympathizers recorded the event in a letter which they wrote to the Governor of Florida:

> At Cape Florida, the Light being within the immediate protection of Key West and most indispensable at this time to the enemy's fleet, as well as knowing it to be useless for us to try to hold it, we determined to damage it so that it will be of no possible use to our enemies. The Keepers at Cape Florida were armed and instructed not to surrender the Light with their lives...The seizure and surrender was made at midnight on the 21st of August, while the two keepers were in the tower, and the iron door below bolted and locked on the inside. We lured the keepers down from the watch room by pretending to have news about supplies they were expecting from Key West. As soon as the door opened, we secured them as prisoners. The party being small, and having only a small Boat to return in, we concluded not to take them prisoners, they professing to be strongly in favor of the South, although they had repeatedly boasted that they would defend the Light to the last...We brought away from the Cape...two Muskets...two Colt Revolvers, and three lamps and burners belonging to the Light.

The men also smashed the central belt prisms of Frow's prized second-order Fresnel lens, rendering it useless as an aid to navigation.

Throughout the Civil War, although the lighthouse was abandoned, Keeper Simon Frow retained his designation as keeper of the Cape Florida Lighthouse. He and his assistant keepers remained at the lighthouse for a while to protect it. With the light out of commission, however, the lighthouse was not considered a further target for Confederate sympathizers, and the keepers finally moved back to Key West. The Frows were back in their snug home in the city when a second daughter, Catherine, was born in 1863.

When the Civil War ended, the Lighthouse Board did everything it could to get the damaged lighthouses back on line as navigational aids. Moving his family back to the Cape Florida Lighthouse, Simon Frow helped as technicians installed the new second order Fresnel lens. On April 15, 1866, he relighted the lamp.

In the summer of 1867, something happened at the Cape Florida Lighthouse which upset the lighthouse authorities. On August 7th, 1867, Keeper Simon Frow was suddenly demoted to second assistant keeper and shipped off to the Dry Tortugas Lighthouse on Loggerhead Key. Frow's assistant keeper, Joseph Copley, had already resigned. To fill the vacancies at Cape Florida, on August 9th, the lighthouse authorities called back into service the seventy-five-year old Temple Pent, Sr., who had served as principal keeper of Cape Florida in the early 1850s.

The Frow presence at Cape Florida, however, would continue as Simon Frow's 27-year-old son, John W. Frow, was appointed to be Pent's assistant keeper. John Frow had been born in Key West in 1840 and had possibly started his lighthouse service at the age of 24 as an assistant keeper at the Tortugas Harbor Lighthouse on Garden Key in the Dry Tortugas. Now, three years later in 1867, he arrived at the Cape Florida Lighthouse, with his wife Adelaide, to serve as first assistant keeper.

The Cape Florida Lighthouse today.

Simon Frow had hopes that his banishment to Loggerhead Key would not be long as Keeper Pent's health was not good. By the early spring of 1868, Pent was back in Key West, where he died on March 10, 1868.

The Keepers Frow:
The Return Home

Stationed at the Dry Tortugas Light Station, Simon Frow was not a happy man. Although most of his family was back in Key West, only 65 miles away, he dreamed of returning his family to the Cape Florida Lighthouse where they could all be together once again. Fortunately for Frow, circumstances would soon make his dream a reality.

When Frow learned that the Cape Florida keeper, Temple Pent, Sr., had returned to Key West and had died, Frow must have known that his son, then serving as the assistant keeper at Cape Florida, would be the best candidate for the new principal keeper at Cape Florida. Simon had not been happy during his eight months of service "on the rock" of the Dry Tortugas away from his family, and he quickly resigned from the United States Lighthouse Establishment to re-establish his family at Cape Florida and to give his son a hand at the old "homestead" lighthouse. On April 25, 1868, the Lighthouse Establishment made it official, appointing John W. Frow as principal keeper and his 60-year-old father, Simon, as first assistant keeper. At the same time, the second Simon Frow son, Charles E. Frow (born in Key West in 1844), arrived to serve as second assistant keeper. Cape Florida Lighthouse was once again firmly a Frow family establishment.

Catherine Sophia Frow (Roberts) was born in Key West on November 13, 1863, the last daughter and child of Simon Frow. At the age of four, she moved with her family to the Cape Florida lighthouse. Living until the ripe age of 94 years, dying on September 1, 1957. "Aunt Kitty," as Catherine was known, left behind her remembrances of her family's life at the Cape Florida Lighthouse.

The little girl was first struck with the long rows of white stakes which marked off lots and streets

A sketch of Cape Florida Lighthouse ca. 1860

for a planned development on Key Biscayne near the lighthouse. She did not know who bought the lots, but it didn't matter. The land where the lots were soon washed away.

One of the things she remembered best was the visits from the Indians. It had now been ten years since the Third Seminole Wars, and the Indians were once again friendly with the local Miami-area settlers. Catherine remembers many times when the Indians would row their long, dug-out canoes from Coconut Grove to the lighthouse to trade for items which the Frow family purchased in Key West. One time, seven canoes came out at once. The Indians traded salted venison, turkeys, deer and raccoon skins, sweet potatoes and corn. In return, they got sugar, flour, meal, shoes, clothing, beads, and tobacco which they loved.

"My, it was good to have their visits," Catherine remembered, and in celebration, the Frows would treat the Indians to a large feast. The Frows had a large cart by which to transport the cargoes back and forth from the light station to the canoes at the bayside landing. In appreciation, when the cargoes had been loaded, the Indians would give the Frow children rides in the cart all around Cape Florida. Simon Frow often read the Bible to the Indians, and "Little Tiger," son of the Seminole chief, called Simon Frow's God, "The Big Man."

The only doctor in the area was an Indian medicine man known as Dr. Jimmie, "and he was pretty good, too," Catherine remembered. Catherine's niece, Josephine, became very ill and almost died at the lighthouse, but the kindly medicine man brought some special cooked herbs, and the little girl recovered. "Lots of the early settlers owed their lives to Dr. Jimmie," Catherine said.

The only trouble they ever had with the Indians was when a man from Lemon City named Bill Smith told the Indians that the government

A photograph of the Cape Florida Lighthouse soon after the Frows lived there.

was sending down a warship to take all the Indians away. He tried to scare the Indians away so he could claim and homestead their land. The Indians were worried and angry. Nineteen canoes suddenly appeared at the lighthouse one day. When Keeper John Frow came down to greet them, the Indians threatened to go on the warpath and kill him. Keeper Frow explained to the Indians that Smith had lied to them, and he succeeded in quieting them down. To help calm the fears and anger of the Indians, Keeper Frow had to resort to an unusual procedure. "Aunt Kitty" recalled:

"My poor brother had to take a drink with each Indian in the party before they would leave, and there were LOTS of them. When the drinking ceremony was over, Johnnie lay stretched out on the ground. The Indians carried him into the house and put him on his bed and left a guard over him until he felt better."

The mainland was beginning to be homesteaded at Coconut Grove, and occasionally the new settlers sailed over to the lighthouse to trade mangos, key limes, oranges, grapefruit, and avocados for some of the trade goods which the Frows maintained.

According to "Aunt Kitty," the keepers' dwelling at the Cape Florida Lighthouse was a beautiful place. The house had large windows to catch the ocean breezes. The living room, usually called the "parlor" in those days, had a large fireplace which was used only on the colder days of the winter. The family had a small pump organ which Simon's wife played to amuse herself and the family. The men in the family would join in on the violin, flute, and guitar. The Frows were a musical family. Young Catherine sang and danced, amusing even the Indians who clapped their hands with glee at her antics.

The kitchen was a separate building behind the dwelling. In it was a large fireplace–for cooking meats, vegetables and most other foods–and a six-foot oven for baking bread and cakes. The Frows tended a large vegetable garden on Key Biscayne. For fresh water, there was a well near the house which supplied water for the garden and the livestock which the Frows kept. There were a lot of chickens, hence the family was never short on eggs. Little Catherine adopted all the livestock and gave them names.

For drinking water, the Frows relied on a cistern which was filled by rainwater from the roof coming by way of a series of gutters and down spouts. A pipe led into the kitchen where a hand pump drew the water for cooking and drinking. Catherine remembered this water as always cool and refreshing.

Catherine's older brother, Joseph Thomas Frow, did many of the daily chores around the house and made sure that the family had plenty of fish, crawfish, and conchs in various traps from which Simon's wife, Sarah, would select the best and provide them as supper for the family. In the center of Key Biscayne was a freshwater pond around which was a major bird rookery. This was also a great source of food for the Frows.

The birds included flamingoes. Catherine remembered that the men took only the mature birds and usually at molting time when the birds had shed so many feathers that they could not fly. They took only what they needed and not a bird more. Catherine remembered that the flamingoes tasted like roast goose. She saw hundreds of flamingoes. They were a beautiful sight, especially when the flock would take wing for a day of foraging.

The Frows also walked the beach, and from May through November, they could usually find female sea turtles crawling on the beach to lay their eggs. Sometimes the Frows would catch a turtle after she had laid her eggs and enjoy turtle soup and steak to augment their diet of meat.

The main meal was eaten at noon and the lighter meal in the evening. This was done so that the dishes and pots could be cleaned and everything set back to order before darkness fell. They had kerosene lamps for lighting at night, and the Lighthouse Board furnished them with a 225-gallon tank of fuel for the tower lamp and personal use. Strict records as the use of the oil for either purpose had to be carefully kept to prove that the keepers were not using too much for personal use or possibly selling off some to visitors.

John, Simon, and Charles Frow did the duties regularly demanded of lighthouse keepers. Just before dusk, they first filled 5-gallon cans from the 225-gallon kerosene tank. Then they carried the smaller kerosene cans up the 122 steps to the top of the lighthouse to fuel the wicks of the large, circular Argand lamp at the center of the Fresnel lens. First, a lens cover was removed from the nearly eight-foot tall second-order lens. Then, curtains, which protected the lens from the heat of tropic sun coming through the glass of the lantern, had to be taken down. The lamp fuel reservoir was filled with filtered kerosene.

Finally, the lamp in the great lens was lighted. There were three wicks in the lamp, and each had to be hand-lighted from a smaller lamp, the inside wick first, and the outer one last. A glass chimney was set over the burning wicks, and then the wicks were adjusted until a 2-inch flame was produced. Now, the second-order lens, nearly 8 feet tall, could produce a light of 12,000 candlepower, extending some 18 miles out to sea.

With three keepers and the light at 95 feet high, one man was always stationed at the top of the tower throughout the night. A clock with an alarm would tell when the next watch was due. A couple of times during the night, a rod-lamp would be hung inside the lens and the main lamp burner shut down so that the wicks could be trimmed. Then, the main lamp was relighted, and the rod-lamp was taken down. At all times, there would be a light inside the lens.

In the morning at sunrise, the lamps would be extinguished and the curtains reinstalled. The lamp would be cleaned and the wicks trimmed, and then the lens would be dusted down and cleaned. The lens cover would be reinstalled over the lens to keep dust and debris from falling on it. Once a week, the bronze framing of the lens would be polished with red rouge and the glass was cleaned with "spirits of wine" or vinegar. Physical maintenance and painting of the lighthouse and the other station structures managed to keep the three Frow men busy.

A sailing vessel would stop by with mail from Key West about every two months. On one occasion, much to little Catherine's delight, the vessel dropped off a young lady with an English accent. She would be the school teacher for the three young children then of school age on the station. She brought with her all the books and necessary supplies, all furnished, as was her salary, by the government for such remote light stations.

Simon's second son, Charles, served as second assistant keeper. His wife, Mary Roberts Frow, had lost three babies due to the coarseness of wilderness births. With his wife expecting a fourth baby, Charles decided to send his wife to a hospital in Key West on the mail boat. Unhappily, the mailboat did not keep its usual schedule at that time, and the birth took place at Cape Florida. However, with the help of the other Frow women, this time, the birth was a success, and Julia Bertha Frow was born.

The Charles Frows, however, did not remain much longer at Cape Florida. He resigned from the Lighthouse Establishment in August, 1869. Charles' younger brother, Simon Frow's youngest son, 21-one-year old Joseph Thomas Frow (born 1848), was appointed second assistant keeper at Cape Florida. Charles and Mary, with daughter Julia, moved back to Key West where two more daughters were born. Missing the Biscayne Bay area, Charles and his family moved back to homestead part of the 160 acres of land that Charles' older brother John had purchased the year before at Coconut Grove. Shortly after their return in 1878, Charles was out fishing in the Bay when lightning struck the mast of his boat, and he was killed instantly.

The Keepers Frow:
A New Lighthouse

For more than ten years, since the end of the Civil War, the Frow family had held sway as the keepers of the Cape Florida Lighthouse. John W. Frow was the principal keeper, his aging father, Simon Frow was first assistant keeper, and John's younger brothers Charles E. and Joseph T. had served as second assistant keepers. Their life on the southern end of Key Biscayne, although primitive and remote, had grown into an idyllic life-style with everything that they needed provided by the environment. The members of the family loved their life and their little kingdom at Cape Florida. However, all things change.

In the early 1870s, the United States Lighthouse Board had determined that an iron-pile tower built offshore on Fowey Rocks would be more effective as an aid to navigation than the old, masonry tower on the southern tip of Key Biscayne. The Cape Florida Lighthouse, however, would remain in operation until the new Fowey Rocks Lighthouse was completed. By early 1878, the Frows knew that the end of their present world was coming closer as they watched the new iron tower slowly growing to completion on the southeast horizon, several miles away. It certainly would be a different place in which to live. There would be no more vegetable gardens or livestock. The Indians would be unlikely to paddle out that far into the ocean to visit, and the Frows would miss the flamingoes and the walks on the beach looking for sea turtles and their nests. It would be a different life just a few miles away out on the Fowey Rocks Lighthouse.

Early that summer, when the new lighthouse was completed, all three keepers Frow–Principal Keeper John W. Frow, First Assistant Keeper Simon Frow, and Second Assistant Keeper Joseph T. Frow– transferred over from Cape Florida to the new Fowey Rocks Lighthouse. It is probable that all three participated in the first lighting of the new lighthouse on June 15, 1878.

The three families followed the men and settled down into their new quarters. Simon's youngest daughter, then-fifteen-year old Catherine later remembered the wood-paneled quarters as "spacious," although they truly could hardly be called that.

The new Fowey Rocks Lighthouse where the Frows were the first keepers.

Nevertheless, the families felt that they were well accommodated in the new iron structure. They could still enjoy the pastimes of fishing and collecting crawfish and conch. Catherine remembered that her mother had expected to have to dust the quarters less frequently as they were surrounded by water. She was surprised, however, that so much dust reached the lighthouse on the wind.

The Frow families had not been aboard the Fowey Rocks Lighthouse three months before they were tested by the monstrous 1878 hurricane. Finally, on September 11th after four days, the barometer began to rise. "The gale broke, and the wind came around to the southwest," Keeper John Frow reported. [See "Stormy Weather on the Reef Lights."]

The abandoned Cape Florida Lighthouse where the Frows were the last keepers.

The Fowey Rocks Lighthouse had survived its first test by hurricane. The keepers spent a week cleaning up and making repairs. Soon afterwards, second assistant keeper Joseph T. Frow retired from the lighthouse. It seems that he perhaps had not enjoyed being aboard the lighthouse during the hurricane. He decided to homestead a section of his brother John's 160 acres in Coconut Grove. A new second assistant keeper was needed, and in the fall of 1878, Jefferson Beale Browne was chosen to fill this gap in the "family" at Fowey Rocks. Young Jeff Browne was only 6 years older than the lovely young Catherine, and the family felt that a romance was starting to bloom. However, second assistant keeper Browne was serious about studying law, and when he left the lighthouse eighteen months later, he enrolled in the law school at the University of Iowa. He finished his law degree in only two years and later became Chief Justice of the Florida Supreme Court.

In 1879, after living for a year on the Fowey Rocks Lighthouse, the Frow families were notified that a new regulation of the Lighthouse Board had been adopted prohibiting the families of the keepers from living on the reef lights. The women and children would have to move ashore. The quarters at the reef lights would henceforth be for men only. In late 1879, the Frow families packed up, and moved to Key West to a new house which Simon Frow purchased in the 800 block of Simonton Street.

Principal Keeper John Frow continued at the Fowey Rocks Lighthouse until February, 1880, when he resigned. He had missed his family too much. Since he could not raise his family at the reef light, he would move ashore where he could be with them. John Frow was succeeded as principal keeper at Fowey Rocks by English-born John J. Larner. Larner would serve for more than fifteen years as keeper of the Fowey Rocks Light Station, dying at the station on July 26, 1895.

Simon Frow and Jefferson Browne continued to work together at the Fowey Rocks Light Station. On February 24, 1880, Simon Frow wrote a letter to the Superintendent of Lights in Key West: "Sir: I herewith tender my resignation as assistant Keeper of Fowey Rocks Light-House, wishing to be released as soon as possible as I am sick and unfit for duty. Simmon Frow." Frow and young Jefferson B. Browne both left the lighthouse on March 30, 1880. Frow was succeeded by Robert Hamilton Thompson, a recently arrived second assistant keeper, who happened to be Simon's son-in-law, having married Simon's daughter Julia.

The Simon Frow home in the 800 block of Simonton Street in Key West, ca. 1896. The smaller building to the left is the mercantile shop of Simon's son-in-law, James Carey.

Simon now rejoined his family in Key West. One of the first things he did was to attend the wedding of his youngest daughter, Catherine, to George Livingston Roberts. Simon Frow had smoked cigars all his life. Just before the family returned to Cape Florida in 1866 Simon had been talking to friends on the dock when his cigar burned down and singed his lip. The sore did not heal and turned into a cancer. A doctor operated and removed as much as he could, but twenty years later, the cancer returned, and Simon Frow died in Key West on September 30, 1886. His wife, Sarah Ann Thrift, survived him until November 24, 1895. They are buried together in the City Cemetery of Key West.

In 1877, Simon Frow's eldest son, John W. Frow, principal keeper first at the Cape Florida and then at the Fowey Rocks Lighthouse, had purchased 160 acres of the Beasley Grant along the waterfront of Coconut Grove for $100. He would later sell some of this land to his brother Joseph and to each of his three sisters. In 1880, Keeper John Frow resigned from the United States Lighthouse Establishment and moved ashore, bringing his wife and adopted son (John Simon Hopkins Frow) up from Key West. John worked as a boat builder and a farmer. In 1881, he sold 31 acres to Charles and Isabella Peacock who would build the first hotel on the south Florida mainland. In 1887, John's sister, Catherine Frow Roberts, and her husband and children also moved to Coconut Grove to homestead on land which later became 2830 South Bayshore Drive.

Catherine's husband, George Roberts, built boats and many of the early homes in this part of the Miami area. John Frow moved back to Key West where he worked some years at the U. S. Customs House. His first wife, Adelaide M. Stirrup died in 1892, and the following March, he married Louisa Sawyer. He also missed the life at Coconut Grove, and when he retired from the Customs House, he moved back.

In 1898, Catherine's sister Sarah, and her husband James Carey would sell their mercantile business in Key West and move to homestead in the Coconut Grove area. George Roberts built them a fine home on a bluff along today's South Bayshore Drive. This home stood until the 1960s when it was demolished for a high-rise condominium. The Frow families were coming "home." Today, the Frows are considered one of the most prominent of the pioneer families in the early history of the Miami area. Historian Arva Moore Parks declares that the Frows were "the most influential of the 'genuine pioneers.'"

The Frows, however, suffered their share of tragedy. Charles had been killed by lightning while sailing in Biscayne Bay in 1878. Forty years later, another Frow tragedy would be enacted on the Bay.

When World War I began, the U.S. government built a naval air training camp at Coconut Grove adjacent to the Frow's property. Here, young cadets were trained to fly seaplanes. On Saturday, April 27, 1918, a young aviator got in his plane and was in the act of taking off from the water for another practice flight. The young man could not see and did not know anything was in his path. Suddenly, the propeller smashed into the mast of a little red sailboat. The sails of the little boat were torn to shreds, and the lone seaman aboard the small craft was killed. It was 78-year old John W. Frow, former keeper of the Cape Florida and Fowey Rocks lighthouses.

Joseph Thomas Frow, born October 3, 1848, was the youngest son of Simon Frow. Joseph served as the second assistant keeper at Cape Florida after his older brother Charles had resigned, and also served in this capacity at Fowey Rocks, until he resigned in September, 1878. He moved ashore to raise his family on a part of John Frow's 160 acres of land at Coconut Grove. He started out as a boat builder, but by 1885, he established a coontie plant farm to process starch for sale in Key West. In 1891, he got a land patent of his own. Frow Street in Coconut Grove was named for him. He often helped newcomers build their homes, and in 1891, he helped build Ralph Munroe's home, "The Barnacle," today a state historic site. Joseph Thomas Frow remained a strong member of the Coconut Grove community until his death on August 29, 1921.

Catherine Sophia Frow Roberts, Simon Frow's last child and daughter, the little girl who so well remembered the wonderful years growing up at Cape Florida, lived to a ripe old age, witnessing the tremendous change in the Miami area. "Aunt Kitty," as she was affectionately known to all, lived in her home by the sea for more than seventy years, having two houses blown out from under her by hurricanes. In 1952, when the City of Miami decided that her property should be used for a city park, the city fathers discovered that "Aunt Kitty" was then the oldest living resident and property owner in Dade County. The City of Miami decreed that "Aunt Kitty" should be allowed to live on her property until her death. At the age of 94, on September 1, 1957, Catherine Frow Roberts, the last person to actually have lived at the Cape Florida Lighthouse died. The Frow Dynasty had lasted a long time.

Joseph T. Frow and his eldest daughter Lillian on the porch of the Peacock Hotel in 1883.

Credit for the wonderful information on the Frow family is due to the generosity of Charles Frow of Marathon who allowed me to copy and study the several books on genealogy and family lore compiled by his cousin, Catherine Burst Lowe Lytton and her late husband Eugene R. Lytton, Sr. To them, I express my deepest appreciation for their work in preserving this exciting part of our history.

From Rogue to Keeper: Joshua Appleby

The name of Joshua Appleby might not be on everyone's lips, but it is famous enough in lighthouse history to merit the name on a new Coast Guard buoy tender. This controversial man was also, in effect, the founder of the first white settlement on Key Vaca, the site of today's City of Marathon.

Joshua Appleby was born in Rhode Island on December 5, 1770 (some sources say 1773). He went to sea as a young man, and as early as 1797, he was already the master of ships out of Providence. Joshua married Sarah (Sally) Viall on June 13, 1793, in Providence. A daughter, Eliza Viall Appleby was born to them on January 23, 1795. A year later, Sarah Appleby died. Joshua Appleby prospered, and by 1806, he owned property on Elm Street in Newport, Rhode Island. He soon married his second wife, Mary Forrester (born ca.1769).

By 1820, Appleby was ready for a new challenge, and he decided to sail to the Spanish-held Florida Keys to seek his fortune. The Adams-Onis Treaty of 1819 had already made the cessation of Florida from Spain to the United States a certainty, and Appleby wanted to get in on the ground floor of the development of this soon-to-be American territory.

In the fall of 1820, Appleby sailed south. He landed to settle on Knight's Key at the west end of Key Vaca. Before long, he was joined by four more families. On November 19, 1822, Appleby and John W. Fiveash of Norfolk, Virginia, formally established a new trading and wrecking port and named it Port Monroe in honor of the President. The townspeople erected a flag staff at the center of their new town. A "Notice to Mariners" that appeared in the March 8, 1823, edition of *The Floridian Pensacola*, described the new settlement: "This port . . . has boats and provisions of all kinds to relieve those who may be so unfortunate as to get on the Florida Reef . . . At present there are four families residing at this place; corn, potatoes, beans, onions, cotton and all West Indian fruit thrive rapidly." Appleby soon removed to Indian Key where he was one of the first settlers. Here, he opened another store for trading with the wreckers and new settlers.

Appleby fished and turtled in the local waters while he looked for wrecks to salvage. In 1823, he was accused of conspiring with the commander of a Colombian privateer to run ashore at Key Vaca vessels that the privateer captured. The wrecked ships could then by legally sold as salvage. Commander David Porter, in charge of the new American naval force sent to Key West to prevent such piracy, immediately sent a squad of marines to Key Vaca to arrest Appleby. They put him in chains and sent him to Charleston for trial. Porter had decided to make this a high-profile case to deter others in the Keys from intentionally wrecking vessels. Porter, however, had chosen the wrong person to use as an example, for Appleby had friends in high places. These included Smith Thompson, the Secretary of the Navy, and President James Monroe. In a surprising twist of events, Secretary Thompson wrote to Porter in July, 1824: "As regards the conduct of Joshua Appleby, detained under arrest, it is not expedient to institute against him any further proceedings; his offense does not amount to a positive violation of any law of the United States; you will, therefore, direct him to be forthwith liberated." Porter had lost his case.[18]

Appleby was released, and he returned to Newport, Rhode Island. By 1830, however, he was back in the Keys, living in Key West with his wife. As Appleby had no criminal record, he was granted a wrecking license by the court in Key West, and he returned to the pursuit of that occupation. According to records, he owned the wrecking schooner *Mary Ann*, and was one of the salvagers mentioned in cases in April 1830 and January 1831. Appleby continued his career as a wrecker for several years, and then in February, 1833, his wife Mary passed away. This, plus Appleby's advancing age, probably started him on the lookout for a less strenuous job. A few years later an opportunity came his way for the job that he needed.

In 1827, a new, 65-foot tall, masonry lighthouse had been built on Sand Key. Joseph Ximenez had been appointed its first keeper, but when life at the Dry Tortugas Lighthouse on Garden Key proved to be too remote and difficult for John and Rebecca Flaherty, the keepers there, William Pinkney, the collector of customs for Key West and superintendent of the lighthouses, arranged for a switch. Ximenez would take over at the Dry Tortugas, and the Flahertys would move to the less remote new station on Sand Key.

John Flaherty died in 1830, and Rebecca remained as keeper until she married Frederick Neill in 1834. Mr. Neill was appointed the new keeper, and he and Rebecca remained on Sand Key until they decided to move back north in 1837. The new collector of customs, William Whitehead, was suddenly hard pressed to find a replacement keeper. Although he had never served with the Lighthouse Establishment, Joshua Appleby, now sixty-seven, wanted the relatively less strenuous and safer occupation of a lighthouse keeper. Due to his many years of experience as a sea captain and navigator in the Keys, Appleby got the job.

Joshua Appleby began his new career as keeper of the Sand Key Lighthouse on July 27, 1837. He was paid $600 per year. His life on Sand Key, however, was not always tranquil. Hurricanes struck in 1841 and 1842. In the latter storm, the keeper's house was wrecked, and the lantern of the lighthouse was damaged. All new lantern storm panes and reflectors and lamps had to be installed.

In 1843, Adam Gordon, the superintendent for lights in the district reported that "with these improvements, the light is exceedingly brilliant and powerful." Although it would be more than a year before a new keepers' dwelling was built for Appleby and his new assistant, Gordon provided for the construction of a seawall to protect the foundations of the masonry lighthouse. Gordon called it "a fine piece of masonry." Finally, in the summer of 1844, the new keeper's dwelling was completed. Appleby and his assistant had just settled in when a hurricane struck, washing away half of Sand Key, demolishing the new house, and badly damaging the new seawall. It took another year to repair the wall and build yet another new house for the keepers.

Once again, Appleby moved into a new house. During the following year, things were quiet, and in the fall of 1846, Appleby invited his beloved daughter Eliza to visit him with her eleven year old son, Thomas Forrester Patterson. Coming down from Newport with Eliza was her friend Mrs. Mary Ann Perry Harris and her adopted daughter. With Appleby and his assistant, there were six people living in the keeper's dwelling on that tenth day of October in 1846.

The Sand Key Lighthouse in an 1834 drawing by William Whitehead.

That day had dawned unusually hot and stifling for October, and no one had a clue that a major hurricane had just devastated Havana, Cuba, only ninety miles away. During the day, the waves began to build. That night, storm clouds filled and scudded across the sky while the barometer began to fall rapidly. Part of Appleby's job was to make notations of barometer and other weather readings for entry in the light station journal. He had to have known that the barometer indicated that a major storm was near at hand. As the weather suddenly unleashed a great fury, Appleby undoubtedly remembered that in the previous hurricanes, the tower had survived when the rest of the structures on the island had been washed away. Appleby ushered his four visitors and assistant keeper into the masonry tower for safety. But in the face of THIS storm, it was not to be enough.

Early on the morning of October 11, 1846, the high storm surge waves of the terrifying hurricane pounded Sand Key to pieces, digging down more than six feet into the sand and undermining the foundations of the lighthouse. Suddenly, the brick tower collapsed, and all inside perished, either being buried alive or washed away. Their bodies were never found. The storm also toppled the Key West Lighthouse where fourteen people lost their lives.

The next day, U. S. Navy Lt. William C. Pease wrote that "The lighthouse at Key West and Sand Key washed away, and Key West is in ruins. A white sand beach covers the spot where the Key West Lighthouse stood, and waves roll over the spot where Sand Key was." In his book, *A Sketch of the History of Key West, Florida*, Walter C. Maloney said that the hurricane of October, 1846, "was the most destructive of any that had ever visited these latitudes within the memory of man." This certainly was the case for Keeper Joshua Appleby. He had paid the supreme price: giving his life that others might be safe from the sea.

To honor the memory of this fascinating keeper, the United States Coast Guard named one of its new "Keeper-Class" buoy tenders in his honor. The 175-foot USCG cutter *Joshua Appleby* (WLM-556) was commissioned on August 8, 1998. The *Joshua Appleby* is home-ported in St. Petersburg, Florida. During the National Lighthouse Conference in October, 1999, she was to transport the conference participants out to Sand Key to view the new lighthouse which replaced Appleby's tower in 1852. The voyage was canceled by the arrival of Hurricane Irene.

The new Coast Guard Buoy Tender "Joshua Appleby."

Carysfort Reef Light Keeper Curry:
Tragedy at the Old Seven-Mile Bridge

In late October, 1919, William Hiram Curry, Principal Keeper at the Carysfort Reef Light Station packed a few belongings, some mail, the monthly station reports, and some food into the station sailboat for his quarterly leave in Key West. He had been on the sea-swept, iron-pile lighthouse for three months, and now it was his turn to finally enjoy some time with his family in Key West, deliver his lighthouse reports to the District Commissioner there, and mail some letters written by him and his two assistant keepers. Curry soon got in the boat, set the sails, and headed off with the prevailing easterly breezes for Key West, 110 miles to the southwest.

It was not a daunting voyage for this keeper who had done this many times since he had become the principal keeper at the Carysfort Reef Lighthouse in 1915. With good winds, he could make the long trek in only three to four days. The trip down to Key West was pleasant, and Keeper Curry may have had time to reflect on the joys of his life.

William Hiram Curry, like so many other Keys lighthouse keepers, had been born in the Bahamas on December 24, 1864, a Christmas Eve present to his parents. The boy loved the sea and gained in maritime skills as he grew up. Then, probably in his twenties, he emigrated to the Florida Keys. He settled in Key West where he married and began a family. Then, like a number of other men in Key West where the local district headquarters of the Lighthouse Establishment was located, he sought to improve the stability of his family's income with a government job with the United States Lighthouse Establishment.

In the late spring of 1893, William Curry applied for a position of lighthouse keeper, was accepted, and took his oath of office. He was appointed to succeed Gideon S. Lowe as second assistant keeper at the Alligator Reef Lighthouse off the southern end of Upper Matecumbe Key. At this light station, not far from and in view of historic Indian Key, Curry would serve under Principal Keeper Edgar J. Russell. When Second Assistant Keeper Curry began his lighthouse service on July 19, 1893, a magnificent painting of his lighthouse was at that moment on public display at the great Columbian World's Fair Exposition in Chicago, celebrating the 400th anniversary of the first voyage of Christopher Columbus.

The Lighthouse Board's exhibit at the great fair included the notation that the Alligator Reef Lighthouse was "one of the most efficient lights on the coast." The three keepers at the Alligator Reef Lighthouse took great pride in this honor. Curry served at this lighthouse, at a beginning salary of $490 per year, for almost four years, being promoted to first assistant keeper there on August 16, 1895, when his pay was raised to $510 per year.

Alligator Reef Lighthouse

On July 1, 1897, Curry was promoted again, this time to first assistant keeper at the Sanibel Island Lighthouse. Although at that time a wilderness location, this was a desirable duty station for Curry and his wife and infant daughter could live with him right at the station. Two years later, however, his then 3-year old daughter broke her arm severely and needed professional emergency treatment. Keeper Curry flagged down a boat carrying cattle from the loading dock at Punta Rassa to Key West, and Curry's wife and daughter boarded it to rush the little girl to the hospital in the "Southernmost City." Curry's wife, upset with the isolation on Sanibel Island, said she would never return there from Key West. Curry decided he had to leave the Lighthouse Establishment to re-establish his family at Key West, and he resigned on June 30, 1899.

Sanibel Island Lighthouse

On September 28, 1901, however, Curry was back in service, this time as second assistant keeper at the Sombrero Key Lighthouse off Key Vaca, under Principal Keeper Rudolph Reike. Later, after John Watkins had become Principal Keeper, Curry, on December 2, 1905, was promoted to first assistant keeper at Sombrero Key. His salary was increased to $600 per year.

On July 1, 1910, William Curry, at age 46, finally had his big break. He was promoted to the rank of Principal Keeper at the American Shoal Lighthouse, south of Sugarloaf Key. He was now completely in charge of his own light station. While he was at this reef light, he oversaw the installation of the latest technology in lighthouse illumination, the new incandescent oil vapor lamp, which burned vaporized kerosene on an asbestos mantle in a process similar to that used in today's Coleman camp lanterns. This new lamp was twice as bright as the old kerosene lamps and used less fuel.

Sombrero Key Lighthouse

After five years at the American Shoal Lighthouse, Curry was appointed to command the Carysfort Reef Light Station. This was the oldest of the reef lights, having been completed in 1852, and the position was one of great prestige. Curry took great pride in his light station, and during the next several years, he held the lighthouse commissioner's "Efficiency Star" for three years for having the best maintained and operated light station in the Seventh District which ran from Hillsboro Inlet on Florida's east coast to Egmont Key on its

American Shoal Lighthouse

west coast. This was a very high honor for the lighthouse keeper.

Yes, William Hiram Curry had had a great career and was considered one of the finest principal keepers in what was then called the United States Lighthouse Service. Now, in early September, 1919, his leave at Key West with his family was coming to a close. Despite a severe toothache, he packed his clothes, picked up dispatches and the pay checks from the District headquarters, collected the supplies and mail, and once again loaded his small sailboat for the voyage back up the shoreline of the Florida Keys, 110 miles to the Carysfort Reef Lighthouse. The trip back was usually more difficult and took more days as Curry would be going against both current and the prevailing winds. His boat did have a small, inboard engine, and going back, he might even have to use it, although it was a matter of pride among the keepers to use as little fuel as possible.

Early on the morning of Friday, September 6th, Keeper William Curry began the long trip back to his lighthouse. His progress was slow against the prevailing winds. On the afternoon of

Carysfort Reef Lighthouse

September 8th, Curry decided to anchor for the night in the lee of Boot Key near Marathon. With a strong wind out of the east, Curry was on the west side of the Boot Key harbor entrance, near the east end of the old Seven-Mile Bridge. After getting secured, Curry probably enjoyed watching as Henry Flagler's East Coast Railway trains traversed the magnificent bridge.

Miguel Fabal, Principal Keeper of the Sombrero Key Lighthouse was familiar with the boats that the Lighthouse Service used in the Keys. Now, high in the lantern of the Sombrero Key Lighthouse, five miles away, he was able to make out with his spyglass the "No. 2" on the bow which identified the boat as being from the Carysfort Reef Light Station. Fabal watched as Curry anchored and approved of his anchorage location with regard to the winds at that time. There was no ordinary indications at that time that a change in the weather was brewing.

In the afternoon of Monday, September 8, 1919, all light stations connected by telephone were advised of the proximity of a hurricane approaching the Florida Keys. When Fabal got his phone call, he and his assistants began preparing to batten down for the storm. Fabal decided to try to reach Marathon by telephone to have someone go out and warn the Carysfort Reef Light Station boat that the hurricane was coming, but the line had gone dead and he was unable to make the connection.

At sundown, the keepers at Sombrero Key could still see Curry's boat anchored to the west of Boot Key with the railroad bridge right behind him. At 9 p.m. that night, the wind began to increase, and by daylight of the 9th, it was blowing 80 miles per hour and increasing. The keepers, using their spyglasses, looked in vain for Curry's boat, but it was nowhere to be seen. Boat No. 2 would not be seen again until it was found floating bottom up several days later, twenty-five miles north in Florida Bay from where it had last been seen.

When the boat was found, the mast had been broken off and was missing, the sail was gone, all standing and running rigging was missing, and the tools, lights, and everything moveable was washed out of it. The rudder was damaged, and the stern showed evidence of having struck something. Keeper William Curry had vanished.

The boat was found by a fisherman who towed it to his home on Cape Sable near Flamingo. The man put new batteries in the boat and the engine started immediately and ran well until it was shut down. The man contacted the Lighthouse Service office in Key West which directed him to tow the boat to Miami for repairs at Pelsang's Shipyard.

The Lighthouse Service waited for thirty days to learn word of Keeper William H. Curry, but the keeper never again was heard from and finally was presumed to have drowned in the hurricane. From the evidence on the boat, two scenarios were derived to explain the keeper's disappearance. First, it may have been that when the weather became very rough from the south, Curry had hauled up his anchor in the hopes of getting through the Seven-Mile Bridge to calmer waters in Florida Bay north of Key Vaca. In the other case, the rough water may simply have parted his anchor cable. At any rate, Curry's boat was swept by the winds and very strong currents through the low, steel spans of the Seven-Mile bridge, sheering off his mast, overturning his boat in the foaming sea and smashing its stern and rudder against a piling. As the storm struck at night, it is possible that Curry was asleep and never had a chance to start his engine or to get his boat under control before it was already too late. The hurricane of September 8-9, 1919, and the Seven-Mile Bridge snuffed out the life of William Hiram Curry. He was 55.

In an October 17, 1919, letter to George Putnam, Commissioner of Lighthouses in Washington, D.C., District Superintendent William Demeritt wrote from Key West:

[Keeper Curry's] entire service extended over a period of 23 years, 10 months, and 20 days. Mr. Curry was a very efficient keeper, and at the time of his death he had been holding the Commissioner's Star for three years, and one of the stations where he was formerly on duty was awarded the efficiency pennant. This keeper was one of that class of old reliable and efficient keepers whose one thought is of their station, and whose greatest pleasure is in maintaining it at the highest degree of efficiency in appearance and operation, and his death is a distinct loss to the District and the Service.

Keeper Curry had an excess of leave time which would not have been erased until January, 1920; however, William Demeritt had a special request of the officials in Washington. "In view of the long faithful services rendered by the deceased it is recommended that this office [Key West] be authorized to pay the widow the salary due Mr. Curry from September 1st to 8th inclusive; amounting to $32.60."

Author's Note: Thanks to Faye García, Chris García, and lighthouse historian Neil Hurley for the information and documents which provided the facts for this story.

Strictly for the Birds —
The Sand Key Lighthouse

There was an earlier lighthouse on Sand Key, built of brick and mortar in 1827, but this lighthouse was demolished in the devastating hurricane of October 10, 1846. It was replaced by a lightship, the 140-ton *"Honey,"* until a new lighthouse could be built.

Upon its completion in the summer of 1853, the new Sand Key Lighthouse received the very first Fresnel lens installed in a lighthouse in Florida, and, after the first five days of illumination, which started on July 20, 1853, Meade installed his own design for a lighthouse lamp which far surpassed the old French lamp used in all American lighthouses previously. Because of the innovative engineering of its design, because of its early use of the French Fresnel lens, and because of its national debut of the Meade hydraulic lamp, the Sand Key Lighthouse has been listed on the prestigious National Register of Historic Places, one of only two reef lights to be so listed.

One of the keepers of the Sand Key Lighthouse played an important role in the early history of the environmental movement in the Keys and in this country. Charles G. Johnson was born somewhere in Florida, but the actual location and the date of his birth (probably sometime around the time of the Civil War) have been lost in the records. We do know that Charles G. Johnson joined the United States Lighthouse Establishment on June 4, 1892, when he was appointed second assistant keeper at the Carysfort Reef Lighthouse off the northeastern end of Key Largo. Apparently, proving himself capable, after only three months, on September 1st, when first assistant keeper William W. Baker resigned, Johnson was appointed to this position. His pay would increase from $490 to $510 per year.

Sand Key Lighthouse in 1907 with the new weather station to the right. Could that be Keeper Johnson in the Boat House?

After seven years of exemplary service, Charles Johnson was appointed Keeper at the Sand Key Lighthouse on September 1, 1899. It took him a month to settle his affairs and move his family from the tiny settlement at Key Largo to the bustling port city of Key West, and he entered on his duty on October 1st. This was a big promotion for Keeper Johnson, and he was now paid $800 per year. Here, Charles Johnson would hold sway as chief commander until sometime after 1912, but he would have more to command than just the lighthouse.

Although storms and shipwrecks were a part of the story of all of the Keys reef lights, at Sand Key wildlife also played an important role, especially the birds. During the 1800s, great numbers of roseate terns, least terns, and sooty terns had come to nest on Sand Key in March. However, by the time Keeper Johnson came on the scene in 1899, the population of the birds had greatly diminished. Johnson was alarmed by the stories he heard from friends in Key West as to the decline in the birds, and he wrote to William Dutcher, chairman of the American Ornithological Union, to see if there was anything he could do to stop the plunder of the birds' nests by the local people, who considered the eggs as quite a delicacy. Johnson wrote that the small eggs had a "rich flavor more so than larger eggs ...and the keepers used to get them by the baskets for their friends in Key West." He reported that "nine to twelve thousand birds used to nest on Sand Key, but so many eggs were taken only two to three hundred young ones hatched."

At the same time, elsewhere in south Florida and in the Keys, plume hunters were decimating the populations of herons, egrets, and roseate spoonbills to supply the lucrative demand for plumes and feathers for ladies' hats, and the depletion of these bird populations was receiving national attention. In 1903, President Theodore Roosevelt would declare the establishment of the Pelican Island National Bird Sanctuary to help stave off the decline of these shore birds. William Dutcher also tried to do what he could. He formed a Bird Protection Committee and began hiring bird wardens to prevent the wanton destruction of the birds and their eggs. Soon after he received Johnson's letter in 1902, Dutcher hired Keeper Johnson to serve as Bird Warden for Sand Key Island.

Johnson became a conscientious warden and posted signs on the island, warning visitors that the birds and their eggs were protected and not to be disturbed. He sent Dutcher detailed reports on the types and numbers of birds which nested on Sand Key and other local islands. In one report, he wrote: "fishermen, pilots, and sportsmen used to take all of the eggs, but I run them off the island, and I have not allowed one of the nests to be troubled at all...this season we have had no trouble as [people] are fully satisfied they will be punished for any offence...they are all law-abiding and stand greatly in fear of the law."

Sand Key Lighhouse tower before the fire. There is not much left of the small key.

We know little of what happened to Keeper Charles G. Johnson after he left the Sand Key Lighthouse sometime after 1912, but we do know that today, terns no longer nest on Sand Key. Although there is very little of the Key left today, laughing gulls do roost along the shore. When someone does land on the little sliver of sand which is Sand Key today, the gulls quickly take flight with a squawk. However, the Sand Key Lighthouse still watches over the remains of Sand Key and remembers the conservation efforts of one Keeper Charles G. Johnson who tried to save the birds.

Author's Note: My thanks to lighthouse historians Love Dean and Neil Hurley for information contained in this article.

Clement L. Brooks'
Carysfort Reef Remembrances

In 1925 Clement Brooks arrived at the Carysfort Reef Lighthouse as second assistant keeper. The young man was greeted at the landing by the principal keeper, who carried Brooks' luggage up a flight of stairs and into Brooks' room "just like at a big hotel," as Brooks remembered more than fifty years later. Here, Brooks would do his best to make himself at home and be contented.

There was a doorway with an ocean view from each of the three keepers' rooms, and from his room, Brooks could walk through the door and out "onto a circular, bridge-type porch...that went clear around" the lighthouse. From this porch, Brooks could look down thirty feet to where the breakers were "dashing over the coral reefs." It seemed strange to Brooks to live in a circular dwelling, and it took him some time to get used to it. He wrote:

> On the west side of the main room was the kitchen table. We used it for reading. A checkered tablecloth, blue and white, covered it and in the center a large size Holy Bible. On each side of the table was a captain's chair. Very comfortable...against the wall was a double...door library... next to it a two-burner oil stove... then the big iron double doors to the outside... usually open. . . next a clothesline that led to a swing-shelve cooler for eats back of a storage closet for groceries. One thing I liked about the lighthouse, there was never a dull moment... you know that great big ocean never is without a storm. I remember one summer it hailed large lumps...really got cold. I put my Pea jacket on and walked to our lower bridge. When I got to the windward side, I opened my jacket. I could lay on the wind. When you can lay against a strong wind, that's the tail end of a typhoon. I believe it was.

Brooks loved to fish from the landing platform. Fishermen would see him sitting there and would come over for a chat. Brooks got to know most of the local fishermen that way. Sometimes, Brooks or one of the other keepers would invite the fishermen to come aboard the lighthouse for a more prolonged visit.

While Clement Brooks served aboard the Carysfort Reef Lighthouse, his pay was $420 per year as a second assistant keeper. First assistants were paid $520 per year, and principal keepers made $820 per year. Keepers worked ten hours each day, six days a week. They usually spent two months on the lighthouse and one month ashore.

A smiling Clement Brooks proudly poses in his lighthouse uniform.

A World of Transition:
Keeper Edward L. Meyer

Many of us know the feeling of having to be away from family during the Christmas holidays. It is a hollow feeling, and we miss our families greatly. Just before Christmas, 1943, as he was approaching by boat his new command, the Sombrero Key Lighthouse, Chief Boatswains Mate Edward L. Meyer of the United States Coast Guard must have had the same feelings. He had always been a very serious and dedicated family man. He was not happy about this new appointment, but it was wartime, and it was his duty.

Before coming to Sombrero Key, the 46-year-old Edward Lockwood Meyer had had a sterling career with the United States Lighthouse Service. He was born on September 14, 1897, on John's Island, South Carolina. In 1923, he joined the Lighthouse Service as second assistant keeper at the St. Augustine Light Station in St. Augustine, Florida. In March, 1926, Meyer planned to resign from the Lighthouse Service to start a different career, but the young assistant keeper had proved himself so capable that St. Augustine Principal Keeper John Lindquist talked Meyer out of resigning and into continuing his career with the Lighthouse Service.

Keeper Edward Meyer

Only a month later, in April, 1926, Meyer was appointed the first assistant keeper at the Mosquito Inlet Light Station. That station near Daytona Beach is today known as the Ponce de Leon Inlet Light Station. With Meyer were his wife, Ellen Mary, his two young sons, Edward, Jr., and Jack, and daughter Betty. A second daughter, Gladys, was soon born. Meyer was a very conscientious keeper and was frequently commended and decorated by the Lighthouse Service for his heroism in a number of desperate rescues due to shipwrecks near that dangerous inlet.

In 1930 Meyer transferred to the Jupiter Inlet Light Station, Jupiter, Florida, where better schools could be found for his growing children. Three years later, Meyer took a position closer to the rest of his family when he became principal keeper of the Charleston Light Station on Morris Island. When that light station was washed away in early 1935 leaving only the tower still standing, Meyer became keeper of the Charleston Harbor and Cooper River Lights.

In 1937, Meyer was appointed principal keeper at the Ponce de Leon Inlet Light Station, and he returned to a light station which he had loved better than any other. He was again often commended for his service by the Lighthouse Service and once received a surprise visit from Daniel C. Roper, the Secretary of Commerce. Prospects looked very bright for Keeper Edward L. Meyer.

In the summer of 1939, however, through an executive order by President Franklin Delano Roosevelt, the 150-year-old Lighthouse Service ceased to exist. The duties formerly performed by the Lighthouse Service would now be done by the United States Coast Guard, an organization formed in 1915 which already had too much on its plate and for which the operation of lighthouses would never be a top priority.

At first, not very much changed. The Coast Guard allowed the old Lighthouse Service keepers to either remain as civilian keepers or to enlist in the Coast Guard. Meyer was only 41. He still had a lot of his career ahead of him. He felt his interests would be better served if he enlisted in the Coast Guard, and he did so. On June 6, 1941, Meyer was appointed a chief petty officer.

The attack on Pearl Harbor on December 7, 1941, thrust the United States into war against Japan and Germany, and things changed quickly at the light stations. For Edward L. Meyer at Ponce de Leon Inlet Lighthouse, the changes were drastic. First, his family, and those of the other two keepers had to be moved "off base." Keeper Meyer, however, had to remain at the lighthouse, sharing his house and the other dwellings of the light station with a sudden new horde of young Coast Guardsmen many who had just recently enlisted for the war effort. The transition would be more difficult than Keeper Meyer could ever have imagined.

Because the traditions and character of the Lighthouse Service and the Coast Guard were different, it was inevitable that conflicts would occur. The lighthouse keepers which the Coast Guard inherited in 1939 were men generally of middle-age or better. The sailors in the Coast Guard, however, tended to be men in their early twenties. When these two mixed, it was a clear case of "generation gap" which exacerbated the traditional and operational differences between the old Lighthouse Service and the younger Coast Guard.

Instead of the peace and tranquility that Meyer had enjoyed with his family at the light station, it now seemed that Meyer was suddenly surrounded by the student body of a high school boarding school. Most of the men were young enough to be Meyer's sons, and the transition was a difficult one for him.

Besides the age difference between Meyer and his new colleagues, there were the operational differences of the Coast Guard and the new exigencies of the war-time policies to contend with. It suddenly was a very different world! With the coming of the war, there was a lot of normal tension. Nazi subs were sighted off the coast, burning allied freighters and tankers were seen, and debris and bodies often washed up on the shore. There was the danger of sabotage at the light stations, and security was very strict.

There was, however for Meyer, another kind of tension. Meyer had been brought up in the very strict, formal, and professional atmosphere of the United States Lighthouse Service. It had been this character of the old Lighthouse Service that had made it the finest such organization in the world. For Meyer and the other old-time keepers, duty at a light station was something special. They saw the light stations as essentially their home. They raised their families there, and many keepers stayed at the same lighthouse for ten, twenty, or even thirty years or more. There is little doubt that Keeper Edward Meyer had hoped to complete the rest of his career at Ponce Inlet.

The Coast Guard also had its rules and regulations, but the young men in its service were there just as a temporary duty station. This was not their home, and they knew that they would be soon be transferred elsewhere. To Meyer, the attitude of the Coast Guardsmen was that of boisterous kids, disrespectful of the sanctity and value of service to the light station. Meyer sometimes found the Coast Guardsmen asleep while on duty, and he reported them. They also threw their cigarette butts carelessly around the tower and grounds. On at least one occasion, a lighted cigarette butt thrown from the tower started a fire in a nearby scrub. The men on watch in the tower were ordered not to throw their cigarette butts from the tower any more.

Meyer was exasperated by the young Coast Guardsmen who did not seem to have his spirit of keeping the tower in pristine condition. Often, in the morning, he would find cigarette butts, trash, and dried sputum all over the marble floor at the base of the tower. In the service room, the conditions were not much better, and the men also left shoe marks all over the locker. Then, the young men, even his assistant keeper, became slack in wearing their uniforms while on duty, and Meyer had to order them to do so. One mid-afternoon, the tower watch time-clock, which was attached to the railing of the tower balcony, mysteriously fell to the ground and smashed. It was well known that the men disliked having to punch the clock every thirty minutes to prove that they were awake during their watches, but Meyer treated the incident as an accident and ordered a new clock from the Coast Guard.

From the monotony of the watches and the tenseness of the war alerts, Meyer knew that something had to be done to improve morale among the men on the station. He got permission to build a basketball court. The work relieved the men of some of the routine boredom almost as well as the basketball court would do when it was finished.

Despite every attempt to provide relaxation and diversion for the men, the tensions of the war were hanging heavy over everyone. Meyer frequently had altercations with the younger men. For most of 1943, Meyer had been without an effective assistant keeper, and had to carry the brunt of discipline by himself. Finally, however, Jones A. Pervis, who had served on Alligator Reef Lighthouse when the Great Labor Day Hurricane of 1935 swept the Florida Keys, arrived. Pervis would be the last civilian to serve as an assistant keeper at the Ponce de Leon Inlet Light Station.

It appears the Coast Guard had become unhappy with Meyer's inability to get along better with his younger colleagues, for on December 16, 1943, Chief Boatswains Mate Leonard L. Galloway, who had served with Pervis at the American Shoal Lighthouse, arrived at Ponce de Leon Inlet to relieve Meyer. Meyer would be transferred to the Sombrero Key Light Station in the Florida Keys.

In March, 1943, Meyer had received promotion to Chief Boatswain's Mate, First Class, but he was unhappy about his transfer in December to a new duty station where his family could not join him. They remained behind near the Ponce Inlet station. However, Meyer did enjoy fishing, and he did a lot of it during the short time he was at Sombrero Key, even going out with some of the professional fishing guides in the Marathon area. It was probably at this time when Meyer decided that when he retired, he would open a fishing camp back home at Ponce Inlet.

In the spring of 1944, Meyer transferred from Sombrero Key to the Dry Tortugas Light Station on Loggerhead Key. Here, Meyer would serve out the rest of his time, retiring from the Coast Guard in 1945. Returning to Ponce Inlet to rejoin his family, Meyer did indeed start his new fishing camp which became one of the most famous along the east coast of Florida during the early 1950s.

Meyer lived until October 9, 1957.

Coast Guard Service on Sombrero Key Lighthouse:
Donald P. Bascome

Donald P. Bascome was born in Tampa, Florida, on September 4, 1934. In March, 1954, he married Ann Bravo, and they had two daughters, Karen and Cathy. Between 1955 and 1957, when Mr. Bascome served on the Sombrero Reef Lighthouse, his fellow Coast Guardsmen on the lighthouse were Boatswain's Mate Second Class Bob Strickland from Atlanta, the officer-in-charge, and seaman Cecil Taylor from the east coast of Florida. Later, Boatswain's Mate First Class Harold Dunbar served as the officer-in-charge. Mr. Bascome enjoyed serving in the Marathon area and has many more memories of the town in the 1950s. Today, Mr. Bascome lives in Tampa, Florida. I feel it would be best if Mr. Bascome tells the story in his own words, and this is it:

The U. S. Coast Guard in 1955 was a branch of the military that few people knew anything about with regard to its mission or what it had accomplished in its history.

I joined the reserves because one of my friends belonged and asked why I didn't join. It was a good way to make a few extra dollars each month being as I was a newlywed. After attending meetings for a year, I decided to go on active duty and get my military behind me, as I was of draft age, and my employer was afraid I would be drafted after he sent me to school.

The only way one could go on active duty in the Coast Guard was to have received your draft notice. This was because their quota was filled. Anyway, in a short time, I was on my way to Groton, Connecticut, with my wife in our 1950 Plymouth to go to Engineman School. After the school was finished, I went back to Miami for reassignment on the CG Cutter *Bramble* temporarily for a trip to Cape Mala to resupply the crew. After returning to Miami, I was on my way to the Florida Keys to a lighthouse called Sombrero Key off of Marathon.

After a 45-minute ride in the station's 23-foot whaleboat, I stepped aboard Sombrero Light. My first question was how old is the thing? At that time, it was nearly 100 years old, but appeared to be in pretty good shape. The previous engineman had already been transferred, so what I learned about the generators and all the rest of the equipment was from the officer in charge, the seamen, and what manuals I could find about the 2.5 KW Kohler generator, and the bank of batteries. Ironically, the first night I was on board, the generator blew a fuse in the starting circuit, and the light ran off the batteries all night. After looking, reading, and a little bit of blind luck, I found the fuse and had it up and running. All the manned lights in the Key West group checked in by radio three times a day. This was to report the arrival or departure of any personnel to or from the light. Also any parts order, or report or any problem on board.

Settling into a routine, I set up a maintenance schedule on the two generators, batteries, boat engines, boat hoisting engine, saltwater pumps, and the light and lens.

On my last visit to Key West in 1997, it was quite a thrill to see the beautiful Fresnel lens that we had cleaned so many times. We even kept the brass framework polished. I was glad to see it on display at the Key West Lighthouse Museum for everyone to enjoy. There were many old artifacts stored in the storage area under the main dwelling. I often wonder what happened to them. [Note: Many of these items were probably washed away when the lower platform of the lighthouse was destroyed by Hurricane Donna in 1960. - T.W.T.]

The house part of the station consisted of five rooms. 1. Crews quarters, 2. Engine room, 3. The kitchen, 4. The officer in charge's quarters and office, 5. There was a bathroom with a saltwater flush tank on the roof. The quarters of the officer in charge had weather instruments and the entrance to the tube which contained the spiral stair to the top.

At the top was the lens room, with three red sectors, and the timing mechanism for the light's group flash. It was a beautiful sight from the top. The water was so clean and clear it seemed you could see everything on the bottom. This lighthouse is about five miles out, located on the inside of Sombrero Reef. In those days on a low tide, the rocks would be protruding out of the water. When a southeast wind would blow long, steady, and strong, the sea would build to enormous waves coming across the shallow water, and would break on the reef, broadside to the boatfalls. This created a serious problem when raising or lowering the boat, and on several occasions when returning to the light, we would have to unload the groceries via a basket, then take the boat back to Marathon to stay until the wind and sea died down.

Approaching Sombrero Key Lighthouse, 1955. Note the lower platform and the water and fuel storage tanks suspended from the second platform (dwelling floor). (Photo courtesy of Donald Bascome.)

On one occasion, I was maneuvering the boat to unload groceries when the basket caught under the roof of the cabin. The procedure was to run in under the catwalk while the two smaller waves passed, and get out into deeper water before the third one came in, which was always the big one. The seaman was trying the get the basket loose, when I yelled at him to hurry up. Here comes a big one! This third wave was very big, and when it hit head on, I fell back and the stern of the boat went under, and as I looked up the bow was pointing straight at the top of the light! Why it did not go over on it's back, I'll never know, but I can still hear the water rushing around me as the stern went under. Luckily, the engine didn't drown out, and we were able to pump out the bilge. Needless to say, the boat went back into Marathon. We lost about $60.00 worth of groceries to Sombrero Reef, but nobody was hurt.

Ike Seigler, who had a boat rental dock, allowed us to tie up when we came to Marathon. He had a young man named Dick Tracy, who worked for him cleaning boats and loading them for renters. They were both great guys. On one trip out to the light, I was by myself when about two miles out, a heavy sea fog rolled in. I couldn't see the bow, it was so thick. So I stopped the engine and threw over the anchor. It wasn't too long before I could see the light in the distance. The guys on board were getting nervous when I finally came into view.

On beautiful, calm days, we did plenty of snorkeling, fishing, and lobstering. During my two years on Sombrero, there were several occasions when we put the boat over to rescue boaters who had capsized in rough water. Sometimes, their boats would float away while diving, or their vessels would become disabled due to mechanical failure.

Looking up at the tower. Note the dwelling house. (Photo courtesy of Donald Bascome.)

The Coast Guard Cutter *White Sumac* would bring us water if we were running low, and gasoline for the generators. I think the guys from the ship were glad to leave when the delivery was completed. Television reception from Miami was poor at best, but Cuban stations came in very good. The only problem was we couldn't understand what they were saying.

Our liberty allowed six days off for twenty-four days on duty. I would always travel to Tampa to be with my wife. This usually involved hitchhiking to Miami, and then a commercial flight on to Tampa. In those days, rides were plentiful when you were in uniform.

During my tour of duty on Sombrero, I had no idea about the history of the reef lights, or who Lt. George G. Meade was. It has only been in the last few years that so much information about the lights has been uncovered. All in all, I can say I am proud to have served. Even though we are called "switchies," I would do it all over again.

[Note: "Switchies" refers to men who served the lights after they were electrified and the electric lamps were turned on by switches. On the other hand, earlier keepers who tended the wicks of the old kerosene lamps were called "Wickies." - T.W.T]

Introduction to
the Appendix

by Gail Swanson

It is extraordinary that two historians of the Florida Reef lights lived in each other's lifetimes - Love Dean and Tom Taylor. Taylor admired Dean and told me often, "she inspired me to do proper research." Both lived on the Keys and spoke at a meeting in Key Largo that Tom organized and I attended January 20, 2002. I had no idea at that time I would be writing in January, 2005 this: that we lost both our reef light historians the same summer, in 2004.

Dean, a former charter boat captain of the Keys knew her Keys lighthouses well, and researched thoroughly, and produced the first monograph of the subject in 1982: *Reef Lights, Seaswept Lighthouses of the Florida Keys.* She revised and expanded her book in 1992 and 1998: *Lighthouses of the Florida Keys.*

I found this e-mail exchange between the two in Tom's papers after their deaths:

July 8, 1999

Love: I will be at this e-mail address for the next five days, then I will be off to do some wilderness camping and hiking in Maine.

Tom: Have a great time in MAINE!!! It was my home for 20 years, and I miss it dreadfully this time of year!! Especially Monhegan Island where I used to play around the lighthouse there and pretend I was the lighthouse keeper. Please breathe in that wonderful balsam fir air for me and that spectacular sea air. It still seems different than the sea air down here for some reason. BEST WISHES!!!

I don't know if there will ever be any more books on the lights of the Keys and the Florida Reef (although my co-editor, Neil Hurley, has written a book on the lighthouses of the Dry Tortugas, *Lighthouses of the Dry Tortugas, An Illustrated History* (1994) and hopefully will write more). Considering that, I have added the following articles and source materials that should be published. I believe this volume is the right place.

This material on beacons, lightship keepers, and lighthouses of the Keys is arranged in chronological order.

1822
Matthew C. Perry's
Request for Lighthouses

Love and Tom had written separately that "commercial interests" were the impetus for building the lights and lightships to protect sea traffic from the dangers of the Florida Reef tract. But the suggestions in the following document came from a naval commander, who recommended solely lights built on land. I discovered this document in 2004 in Matthew C. Perry's letterbook at the National Archives. Politically-correct Perry had re-named Key West "Thompson's Island" for the Secretary of the Navy, and the port for John Rodgers, President of the Naval Board.

G.S.

Portions of a Report to Secretary of the Navy Smith Thompson from Lt. Cmdr. Matthew C. Perry
U.S. Schooner Shark
Port Rodgers, Thompsons Island
March 28th, 1822

I may be excused in taking this opportunity of suggesting through you forward to the Honb. Secy. of the Treasury the great avant of Light Houses, on the Florida Keys - The happy transfer of so fair a portion of Territory to the U. States has led to the belief that under the enlightened and liberal policy of our Govmt. the navigation of the shores of Florida will be rendered more safe and convenient. Numberless are the vessels and lives that have been lost on this treacherous coast so common are ship wrecks in the neighborhood that there are many vessels turned wreckers, employed solely for the purpose of rescueing property from destruction of which they receive a very large share as salvage. That rapid current denominated the Gulf Stream sweeps the Florida Reef, with incredible velocity, changing its course at every variation of the wind, thusly baffling the skill of the most experienced navigator and as they are deprived of the common beacons so necessary in the navigation of an intricate coast, so are they exposed to the most imminent dangers. The great number of vessels that daily pass through the Gulf of Florida to and from the ports of New Orleans, Pensacola, Mobile, and the Ports of Cuba, Jamaica, and Spanish main, render the erection of light houses, not only an act of justice on the part of our government but humanity, and a regard to the safety of the lives, and fortunes of our citizens, seriously demand so desireable a measure. I should feel diffident in thus introducing my opinion upon you Sir, were I not fully impressed with the belief, that the subject requires the prompt and serious consideration of our government.

At present vessels bound into the Gulf of Mexico and Mexican Sea are compelled to make the Island of Cuba - for the purpose of shaping a correct course to clear the dry Tortugas (the southern extreme of the Florida Reef) by approaching Cuba they expose themselves to the depredations of the numerous picaroons; that infest the neighbourhood of that island. But if light houses were erected on the Florida Keys - vessels in passing and re-passing through the Gulf might keep on soundings the whole distance, and indeed might find safe navigation inside of the Reef.

As to the number and location of the light houses, I should presume there ought to be four, one on each extreme of the Florida Reef, and the other two at intermediate spaces, say one on Cape Florida, another on or near Key Largo, the third on Sand Key, if it be sufficiently stable, and the fourth on the S. West Tortugas.

1822
Midshipman Joseph Morehead's Suggestion:
A Light on Sand Key

From the same letterbook is a report of Joseph Morehead, a midshipman who, with another crewmember of the Shark, *was left for weeks on Key West to establish occupation by the U.S. The report is excerpted here and there are blanks for words where the script could not be determined.*

G.S.

Thompson's Island, Port Rodgers, July 20th, 1822

From the time I landed on Thompson's Island until the last of May the weather was generally very pleasant....These waters abound with a variety of excellent scale and shell fish and a number of [fishing] smacks are kept employed in the reef catching fish for the Havanna market. This harbour is the principal seat for the smacks and the wreckers employed on the reef...it would be _______ if some attention was paid to their motions, the numerous piracies committed on the Cuba shore _______ merchantmen passing through the Gulf to keep close to the reef, and as this is a difficult and dangerous navigation, in consequence of the variations in direction and force of the currents and the difficulty frequently experienced in distinguishing landmarks, a light house on some prominent point, would afford important advantage in enabling _______ to avoid shipwrecks, and with a new and certain departure to hurry through a part of the sea so much infested by pirates and so full of dangers. Key Strandaway about nine miles S. W. by S. of this harbour appears to me an eligible site for such a work. It is a small sand Key situated on the reef having a rocky base, consequently affords the principal material for a light house.

J. Morehead[16]

"Key Strandaway" is Sand Key, where a lighthouse was built five years later.

G.S.

1826
Protest Against the Schooner *Adeline*:
Trying to Build a Beacon on Looe Key

Key West was officially settled in 1822. In 1825, the year of this event, the Navy abandoned their pirate-hunting station on the island because of yellow fever. The Florida Keys-based wreckers, however, were just getting good at their operations. In 1825, according to testimony in another case, "Key West...[where] a small part only inhabitable...The population at Key West was then about 175 - about 80 of them military - 60 or 70 more black...There was but one house on the island that was comfortable - it was owned by P.C. Greene & Co. & they all lived there...there is no other business but wrecking business done there."[17]

The following document was found to be misfiled by a clerk long ago and was given to me by archivist Bruce Chappel at P. K. Yonge Library of Florida History, University of Florida, Gainesville, in 1991. There are some blanks in this transcript for script that was unreadable.

G.S.

Elias Wallen, contractor for building a beacon on the Island of Looe Key and for placing 5 spar buoys on the Florida Reef on the coast of Florida for the Government of the United States makes and intends this his protest against the Schooner *Adeline*, Capt. E. Kelly, owners and all concerned chartered in the Port of Charleston on the 12th day of November, 1825 by Joseph Tyler as agent for the said E. Wallen, in manner following:

First, that is to say: That the said Schooner *Adeline*, Edward Kelly, Master, didn't carry the whole of the materials designed to be shipped on board of her and which the owners said she would carry putting the said Wallen to a considerable expense in lading and unlading 5000 brick, about 1000 feet lumber and one ____ of water, consequently compelling him out an exorbitant freight to ship said brick and lumber by other vessels, and causing two days delay of the brick and cargo in the Port of Charleston.

Secondly, that the said Schooner *Adeline* was in so leaky a condition when laded and unreadiness for sea as to prevent the said E. Wallen or his agent from being able to effect insurance on the cargo consisting of building materials, provisions and 5 spar buoys and anchors for the same although the said Schooner *Adeline* was warranted in the charter party as being ____ and sound in hull and rigging and in complete readiness to receive the cargo and perform the voyage.

Thirdly, that the said Schooner *Adeline* was not seaworthy being in so leaky a condition as with difficulty to be kept free by all hands, and being deficient in sails, rigging, cables and boats to the great danger of the loss of the vessel and cargo and of the lives of all on board.

Fourthly, that on Sunday the 18th day of November, 1825 when endeavouring to get the mechanics on board from the City of St. Augustine, a part of the duty which the said Schooner *Adeline* was chartered for, namely, to carry the workmen who were to build the beacon on the Island of Looe Key when said schooner was standing off and on the said harbor of St. Augustine she leaked so much that Capt. Kelly deemed it necessary to hold a consultation with his mate and men about eight o'clock at night and it was determined by all hands in said consultation that the said Schooner *Adeline* was not capable of performing said service and if persevered in she must go down as all hands could not keep her free, consequently must bear away for the first harbor so as to save the lives of all on board if possible to the great detriment and disappointment of the said E. Wallen not being able to get his workmen off as he was then under a penalty of executing the work for the United States on or before the first day of January, 1826 in consequence of which the said E. Wallen was then in his own defence compelled to abandon the vessel and cargo to Captain Kelly, the owners, and all concerned as the principal object for which she was chartered namely the taking off from the City of St. Augustine the workmen who were to build the beacon on the Island of Looe Key was thus frustrated. And further the said Capt. E. Kelly and his mate Mr. Lakeman both repeatedly said they informed the owners of the said Schooner *Adeline* previously to her lading in the port of Charleston that she was not in her then present state (being leaky and bad unsound) in a condition to take in a cargo or to perform the voyage without previously undergoing repairs which information was not attended to by the owners.

And the said E. Wallen further protests against the Schooner *Adeline*...that on the second attempt of Capt. Kelly to take onboard the mechanic and workmen of the said E. Wallen, when laying at anchor off the Bar of St. Augustine on Friday the 2nd of December the said schooner parted her cable when there was but little wind from the Northwest in consequence as he believes of the said cable being unfit for service to the imminent hazard of the lives of all on board. And the said E. Wallen further protests against the Schooner *Adeline*...that the said Capt. Kelly did on the 7th day of December sail from Key West with but one cable and was anchored where he could have purchased a cable for $35.00 from Capt. Disney[18] consequently making for additional risk of the vessel and cargo - and the said Wallen further protests ______ against Capt. E. Kelly for getting under way at Looe Key on the 16th day of December, 1825 and running to Key West the wind at Northeast thus prolonging the voyage unnecessarily and contrary to the interest of the said E. Wallen - and the said E. Wallen further protests ____ that in consequence of the Schooner *Adeline* not being able to perform that part of the service for which she was chartered...the said Wallen was compelled to pay Capt. Place of the sloop *Sarah Isabella* $91.00 for their passage to Key West. And the said E. Wallen further protests against the said Schooner *Adeline*...for that on...the 22nd day of December, 1825 at about eight o'clock at night when laying at anchor off the Island of Looe Key she was found dragging her anchor and getting nearer the shore when Capt. Kelly being called from his berth where he had been the most of that day intoxicated. He the said Capt. Kelly after a vain attempt to get the anchor up and make sail did with his own hands and an axe cut the cable contrary to the express advice of his mate and sailors, thus unnecessarily loosing our only anchor. And in a few minutes the said schooner struck on the reef and was stranded near to the said Island of Looe Key where there was still on board of her a cargo consisting of ______ cases of lime, 14000 brick the 5 buoys and 5 anchors for the same and the said Wallen further protests ____ for the want of attention in the said Captain Kelly in rendering assistance to save the cargo still on board which was done by the said Wallen by hiring the mate and sailors together with all the masons and laborers on the island [of Key West] at a very considerable expense...and further for the said Kelly abandoning the said Schooner *Adeline* carrying off all the rigging and furniture he could save from the wreck and also when in Key West for his selling the hull as part and the remaining articles of the said schooner *Adeline* knowing that there was still a part of the cargo on board the consequence was that Capt. Bell the purchaser of said hull was contrary to the express orders of the said Wallen set fire to the said hull for the purpose of saving the old iron which made it more difficult and more expensive to save the anchors for the buoys and brick then on board - and consequence of the loss of the schooner *Adeline* he the said E. Wallen had to employ the Schooner *Mary Elizabeth*, Capt Pent[19] at an expense of $400 for 18 days to anchor the 5 buoys in the Florida reef agreeable to his contract and the United States and to bring home himself and 3 workers to St. Augustine.

And lastly the said E. Wallen protests against Capt. Kelly for his vexatious detention of the Schooner *Adeline* 3 days in the port of Charleston previous to sailing from thence after the mate stated she was in readiness for sea and also for the intemperance by intoxication of said Capt. Kelly at difficult times when the master of said Schooner *Adeline* during ______ the voyage.

This done and protested in the City of St. Augustine this 14th day of July, 1826.

Seven Years Later...

Observation on the Looe Key Beacon

From the log of the U.S. revenue cutter *Marion*, May 3, 1832:

At 10 AM hove too off Looe Key and sent the boat to examine the beacon which was found to be in very bad order the top being blown down for 4 or 5 feet below the single, at noon the boat returned pulled away and stood to the westward.[20]

1827

Carysfort Lightship Crew Witness a Seafight between a British Warship and a Spanish Slave Ship

by
Gail Swanson

On December 17, 1827, the British warship HBM (His Britannic Majesty's) *Nimble* was cruising the Florida Straits to intercept slave ships enroute to nearby Cuba. The slave trade had been banned by law by both Great Britain and Spain, yet the horrid trade in human beings to the Spanish colony of Cuba, a major market, continued despite the laws. The British (and at times, the Spanish) stationed warships to stop the trade by citizens of both nations.

That day the British fired two shots at and boarded a Baltimore schooner, the *Lapwing*, enroute to New Orleans, and at the same time shot at the *Reuben Ross*, enroute to Key West, also from Baltimore, which outran her.

Two days later near Orange Cay, the Bahamas, another vessel was sighted. Apparently the *Guerrero* was sailing from the north down the Florida Straits in attempting to evade the warships patrolling the long northern coast of Cuba. The *Guerrero* had only 250 miles more to sail in her voyage from Africa before reaching the coast near Havana. It was noon. From HBM *Nimble*'s log:

> Sail in sight...Observed stranger to be a suspicious looking brig. I set topsail, cleared for action & fired 2 guns to bring stranger to whom we observed hauling up to avoid us; made more sail.[21]

She was, the British may have thought, one of the Spanish slavers they had been alerted to that sailed from Havana for Africa in July. The pursuit was on. HBM *Nimble* carried a crew of 56, had 8 "guns" (cannon) according to one source but another states "two gunades and an 18 [pounder] on a pivot" and measured 83'7" on her deck, 22'2" beam and 9'5" depth of hold. Later written of her opponent the *Guerrero* was this:

> Her force was sufficient to have blown the Nimble out of water at one broadside - why the Captain...did not do so, may appear strange; but he says he depended upon his vessel's sailing...did not wish to risk the lives of his negroes, when he could escape by superior sailing...[22]

During the first five hours of chasing the *Guerrero* the weather turned bad from a cold front pushing through. The *Nimble*'s log:

> 5:00 Strong breezes and squally with a heavy swell, carrying a heavy press of sail & gaining on chase. Observed her bear up.

> 6:15 Having closed considerably fired a gun to bring her to which was returned immediately by her guns & musquetry. Commenced action.

The events were also later reported in a letter written from Key West, certainly from information given by a member of *Nimble*'s crew:

A sail was reported ahead, to which chase was immediately given, and continued until dark, when she attempted to cross the Nimble's bow, by bearing round up, when at a quarter past six she was brought to action, which was briskly kept up on both sides.[23]

Dusk became night as the ships approached the Florida Reef. The *Guerrero* appeared to be sailing at the rate of ten miles an hour, a very fast sailing ship for the time.

Six miles off Key Largo there was a lightship - stationed by American government one year before, to warn mariners of a dangerous coral reef that parallels the Florida Keys archipelago. Aboard the lightship *Caesar* Capt. John Whalton could see the flash and hear the report of the guns. The battle between the ships was happening just a few miles to the northeast of his lightship.

The hundreds of people jammed in the hold of the *Guerrero* could not have known what was going on above them, why the cannon fire, the gunfire. Nor, in the dark, could Capt. Whalton and his crew have known what was happening.

After 30 minutes of the sea fight the captain of the *Guerrero* pretended to surrender to the British by showing a light. The *Nimble*'s log:

6:45 Ceased firing & hauled up after her...Having regular [depth] soundings from 6 to 4 fathoms [36 to 24 feet] approaching Florida reef.

But more went on than was recorded in the ship's log. The letter writer at Key West revealed a bluff by the Spanish captain:

[The slave ship] having, about a quarter before seven, slackened her fire, she hauled to the wind, fired a blank cartridge, and showed a light to leeward, when the Nimble ceased firing. After having thus apparently struck [her flag, a sign of surrender] the chase made off, and after being again pursued, it was found the Nimble was in 6 fathoms water, off the Florida coast.

The log:
7:30 Observed chase on shore.

Not knowing where in the entire world they were, or what the ship hit, or why, 41 people in the hold perished in the *Guerrero*'s collision with the coral. The slaver's hull tore open. Then the masts fell. There were about 650 people onboard when this happened, Spanish and African, their cries "appalling beyond description."[24] The crew of the *Nimble*, over two miles away, was probably the source of the following account printed in the Bahamas newspaper:

The masts of the chase were heard to fall with a tremendous crash, and a horrid yell from those onboard, which left no doubt of her being a Guineaman.[25]

Reacting to the danger, the British crew tried staying their schooner - trying to go about, to avoid hitting the reef. Five minutes later, at 7:35, HBM *Nimble* also struck the coral.

An anchor was put out in the 4 fathom (24') deep water, the sails furled, ballast and shot were thrown overboard to lighten the warship, but within a half hour her movement in the swells broke the anchor line. HBM *Nimble* drove further onto the reef. Twenty minutes later, she drifted off the reef into 2 fathoms (12'), another anchor was put out, but the warship drifted right back onto the reef. The tide receded. The *Nimble* moved no more. There could be no rescue. It was then about 9:00, and still squally.

President John Quincy Adams would become involved in the drama of the Africans aboard the *Guerrero*. At about that very time, in the evening of December 19, 1827, he was writing the day's events in his diary which coincidentally included: "a resolution asking for the correspondence with the British Government relating to the erection of lighthouses on the coast of Florida."

The lights of the lightship, apparently, had been too weak to warn where the dangerous reef was.

On the wreck of the *Guerrero* 90 ruthless Spaniards in the slave trade and 561 helpless Africans were on a ship off an uninhabited coast six miles from land, in cold and stormy weather, at night, sinking. By morning the ship had turned over onto her side, and was full of water.

Six years before, 1821, the United States received Florida from Spain. The next year a little settlement formed on one of the Florida Keys nearest Havana: Key West. The island had fresh water ponds and a fine deep-water harbor. The economy of the 1 x 3 1/2 mile island was based on fishing for the Havana market - Havana only 90 miles away - and on "wrecking" - that is, saving ships that ran onto the reef, and/or their cargoes, for a portion of their value.

Anchored at Black Caesar's Creek in the Upper Florida Keys about 100 miles from Key West, its occupants hoping for a wreck, were the wreckers *Thorn*, Capt. Charles Grover, and the aptly-named *Surprize*, Capt. Samuel Sanderson. The *Thorn* had eight men aboard, the number aboard the *Surprize* is unknown. The wreckers (a term used both for the vessels and for the men) saw the ships the next morning and Capt. Grover hastened to the scene, getting there by 6:00 a.m. Grover came to the closest ship, the *Guerrero*. He launched his boat and with two men sailed for the warship, leaving orders to his mate to take possession of the slaver.

Upon reaching the grounded warship *Nimble* Grover asked her Lt. Edward Holland if he wished assistance who answered in the affirmative. Then with two British seamen put aboard his boat Grover sailed to the *Surprize* then also at the scene and requested Capt. Sanderson to attend to the *Nimble*. He then returned to his vessel anchored at the wreck of the slave ship.

Lightship keeper Whalton early that morning sailed to the scene six miles from his station with the lightship crew (about six men) and met the *Surprize* towing the *Nimble* off the reef into deeper water. He boarded the *Surprize* to assist the wreckers.

Capt. Grover boarded on the *Thorn* 54 Spaniards and 246 Africans, women first. A fishing smack then arrived on the scene: the *Florida*, Capt. Austin Packer of Key West and Mystic River, Connecticut. Packer boarded 142 Africans and some 20 Spaniards on his schooner, which perhaps measured about 55' x 16' x 7' (the popular size of New England fishing vessels of the time).

Guerrero's captain Joze Gomez saw before him early that morning a warship stuck on the coral rocks some two miles away, $156,000 in human cargo (520 Africans who survived the wrecking worth $300 each in Havana), and three small vessels crewed by American simpletons. These were fishermen, and wreckers, men that moored their ships for weeks and even months at low, uninhabited, rocky and swampy islets, swatting mosquitoes, waiting for someone to have an accident. Gomez commanded a slaver, was a pirate who had stolen his human cargo from other ships off Africa, was a bluffer and then he became a hijacker.

While Grover waited for his "consort" Capt. Sanderson of the *Surprize* to arrive at the wreck from his exertions with the warship, the fishing smack *Florida* set sail, for Key West.

She arrived instead at Santa Cruz, Cuba, near Havana, the first vessel to be hijacked.

At 11:00, delayed because of a necessary repair to a sail damaged in pulling the warship off the rocks, the *Surprize* came to the slaver towing *Nimble*'s boat with Lt. Holland, mate R. H. Elliot, and six seamen in it. All came onboard the *Thorn*. Holland's ship had been freed but she still could not sail for the rudder had broken off. Holland was a man of action, and was anticipating trouble by the slave traders, and did then what he could to ameliorate the situation. His intuition is astonishing, for he then had no knowledge of what was then happening at sea aboard the *Florida*. Nor would he for five more days.

Under his direction the British discharged all the loaded firearms onboard the *Thorn* that had been saved from the slaver and threw others overboard or otherwise disabled them with water. At 12:00 the *Surprize* took aboard the remaining Spaniards, 12, and Africans, 121. Sanderson later related the ordeal of rescuing people from the wreck:

> The sea making...a clean breach over them, the slaves and crews being able to save themselves by holding on to ropes fastened for that purpose, they succeeded in saving all on board.[26]

How some 610 people survived the sea on a ship turned over on her side can perhaps be surmised by Sanderson's relation: they had been hanging from the rigging. It must have been an astounding sight.

The tension was very high. It became clear to all what the disposition of the Spaniards was. They could overpower the Americans. The *Thorn* did not sail for Key West - it was then 4:00 and night would be coming soon. She was anchored next to the warship for the protection of her guns that evening, at the request of Lt. Holland. The *Surprize*, with only a handful of Spaniards aboard, remained near the wreck after another wrecker, her crew armed, arrived and stayed near her. Lightship Capt. John Whalton was terrified from the events of the day he had witnessed. After the *Thorn* left for the warship, he reported,

> I then requested Capt. Sanderson to allow me to withdraw from his vessel as I expected she would be taken by the Spaniards. He acquiesed and I proceeded on board the lightboat.[27]

At a wind change *Thorn's* crew moved her slightly away from the warship to avoid fouling her cable with that of the *Nimble's*, and then at 8:00 the captain and most of the crew, after having given the watch orders to keep a good lookout went into the cabin for supper.

That was all the slave traders needed. Armed with daggers and with a death threat to Capt. Grover they hijacked the *Thorn*. The British fired muskets at them (their cannon had been taken off by the wreckers to lighten her) but the gunfire was ineffective, and the *Thorn* sailed for Cuba. Whalton and his crew may have also heard that gunfire from their normally quiet station on Carysfort Reef. Later Whalton made his way to Key West where he gave a deposition on what he had witnessed, which follows. It is from the Public Record Office in London, where my researcher discovered it in 1992. The descendants of John Whalton, the Joe Whalton family of Big Pine Key, did not know of Whalton's experience and the existence of this document until I gave them a copy of my transcript.

> The deposition of John Whalton, commander of the lightboat *Caesar* at Bason Bank on the Florida Reef, being duly sworn says that on the 19th of December 1827 at 7:00 p.m. I saw the flash and heard the report of 7 or 8 guns.

At daylight in the morning discovered two vessels on shore, one of them a schooner on her beam ends with main and fore sails set, the other 7 or 8 feet above the deck.

Shortly after daylight discovered two sails running down for them. Fitted out my first cutter, beat up towards them. About 6 miles from the lightboat fell in with the sloop *Surprize* with HBM Schooner *Nimble* in tow, commanded by Edward Holland, Esquire.

Shortly before getting alongside her I discovered the schooner from taking a rank shear in consequence of heaving the sloop, to jibe and carry away her main boom. Both vessels then came to anchor. I boarded the sloop Surprize, Capt. Sanderson, and assisted him with my crew to fish his boom; during that time Capt. Holland came on board and requested Capt. Sanderson tow his boat up to the brig. Shortly after, Capt. Sanderson got underway Capt. Holland came alongside in a boat and 10 or 12 men. About 12:00 Capt. Sanderson came to in a short distance and then went to work in his two boats and a boat belonging to the brig with some of the schooner *Nimble's* crew in her and saved the balance of the negroes and crew.

At 4:00 p.m. Capt. Morrison in the schooner *General Geddes* arrived and came to anchor near the wreck. At the same time the schooner *Thorn* got underway, dropped down to the man of war schooner and came to anchor near her. She had on board Capt. Holland and some of his crew. I then requested Capt. Sanderson to allow me to withdraw from his vessel as I expected she would be taken by the Spaniards. He acquiesed and I proceeded on board the lightboat where I remained until the 22nd.

On the 21st in the morning I discovered the schooner *Thorn* was missing from where she was laying the evening before and suspected the Spaniards had taken possession of her and proceeded to Cuba. Took my boat to endeavor to get passage in her to Key West but could not catch her. On the 22nd went on board the schooner *General Geddes*, found her laying to anchor about one cable's length from HBM Schooner *Nimble*, found one man on board, asked him for Capt. Morrison who replied he was on board the man of war schooner with his carpenters and part of his crew fitting a rudder for her.

I sent for Capt. Morrison as I wished to see him. He came on board and informed me the schooner *Thorn* had been taken during the night by the Spaniards and that he and his crew had laid under arms all night guarding the sloop *Surprize*; while on board of Capt. Morrison's vessel the man of war's boat returned twice from the wreck laden with goods. I then told Capt. Morrison if he would give me a passage it would be my duty to come down to Key West and report the transaction to the collector of the port. He did so and we arrived at the aforesaid port on the 24th at night [Christmas Eve] and immediately made my report accordingly.

John Whalton

Signed and sworn to before me this 7th of January, 1828

George E. Tingle, Justice of the Peace[28]

1836
A Chilling, Newly-Discovered
Letter of Carysfort Lightship Capt. Whalton

by Sally Whalton & Gail Swanson

This article was first published in the quarterly journal of the Historical Preservation Society of the Upper Keys, <u>History Talk</u>, Fall, 2003.

G.S.

A letter of John Whalton, the Carysfort Reef lightship captain killed by Seminole Indians on Key Largo has been discovered. South Florida archaeologist Robert S. Carr donated the letter to the Historical Museum of Southern Florida in 1978. In a conversation (with Sally Whalton) Carr said he believes he found it at an antique show in New England, and, since it was written in Key West, purchased it.

The museum library added it to their collection describing it as written by "John Whatton...a soldier stationed at Key West in 1830...during the ongoing fighting with the Indians." One of the authors of this article (Gail Swanson) knew there were no Indian battles in 1830 and copied the letter in 2002, hoping that it was written by John Whalton. That it was probably written by someone other than John Whalton was her initial conclusion. However, upon communication with the co-author, Sally Whalton, it was discovered the letter was indeed Whalton's, for he was writing to Reverend John G. Herman at the Moravian School in Nazareth, Pennsylvania, about the health of his son, Joseph.

Sally Whalton had researched this Pennsylvania connection as early as 1977 (before Carr even found the letter in New England), inquiring of records to the Moravian Archives of Bethlehem, for she had discovered the connection from other source material. The reply from Pennsylvania:

The register of students entering Nazareth Hall is printed, and shows a Joseph C. Whalton of Indian Key, Fla., entering in 1835..., a Stephen R. Mallory was enrolled in 1826, from Thompson's Island [Key West], Fla.[29]

Sally Whalton has even been to the church school attended by her husband's ancestor and young Mallory, the future Confederate Secretary of the Navy. Mrs. Ellen Mallory, mother of Stephen, and Capt. John's wife, Felicia, were neighbors and among the earliest settlers of Key West. The letter follows:

June 16, 1836[30]
[Postmarked from Key West]
Rev. John G. Herman
Nazareth N.H.C. Penn.
Dear Sir,

I this day received three kind letters from you informing me of the state of Joseph' health and illness. I feel truly grateful for your attention to my boy and that of Mrs. H. am truly sorry that you should have to wait so long for your money. I sent a draft to Mr. Burring for 200 dollars and requested him to settle my boy's bill as soon as possible. I have all so made arrangements for the payment of your bills as soon as due. I wrote you on the subject and was in hopes you had received my letters before this.

We are in a dreadful state in the territory at present with the Indians and God knows best how it will terminate. All ready there has been many lives lost and this summer it appears that the few troops that were in the ____(?) has been with drawn so that the Indians it appears are turned loose on the unprotected families of this part of the country. We are perfectly safe at this place as we are at least seventy or eighty miles from the main land. I am in grate haste, you will give my love to my boy. You and your family have my prayers and God's blessings. You must excuse my English.

Yours truly,

John Whalton

Four months before John Whalton wrote the above a 12-year-old boy from St. Augustine wrote of the fears of those aboard the lightship:

January 31, 1836
Tallahassee
My dear Mother,

You must excuse me from not writing a long letter, as I have little to tell you. We had a very pleasant but long passage to Indian Key. We saw several villages on the coast before we reached Indian Key, but they were all deserted, the people of Indian Key were very much frightened under arms and expecting an attack daily. There was a family [named] Cooley just below the lighthouse at Cape Florida murdered by the Indians. And, it was very singular, their mother was almost an Indian herself, and the children were named after Indians and could speak Indian better than they could speak English.

The father had gone to Indian Key and left his family at home as he expected no danger from the Indians. They heard the Indians and attempted to fly, the boy and girl were shot down as they made an attempt. The mother who had an infant in her arms received a ball through her and the infant's body. The father took a canoe and returned in a few days and found them all dead as before mentioned.

There is a light ship among the Keys and the sailors that were aboard were very much alarmed for their safety.

Notwithstanding all the danger that was apprehended at Indian Key, I spent my time very pleasantly.

Mrs. Houseman, the wife of the owner of the island, gave me some coconuts, which I pulled with my own hands off the trees, on the island there are also bananas, papayas, tamarands, and other fruits growing there in abundance.

We also had a pleasant journey from Indian Key to Key West for it is delightful sailing among the Keys. On our way to Key West we also passed some good sized villages, but they were all abandoned on account of the Indians....

Love to all,

Your affectionate son, Edmund K. Smith[31]

On June 23, 1837, a year and a week after John Whalton had written his letter to the reverend in Pennsylvania he and his crew were attacked by the Indians at their garden on Key Largo. Whalton was killed in the attack.

1872
Sabotage on Sombrero Key Light

Tom Hambright, Director of the State and Local History Collection at the Monroe County Public Library, Key West, found this account in the "Dry Bank" (Sombrero Key) Lighthouse keepers' log at the National Archives. It is now a part of the library collection. The settlement referred to, Hog Key, was (before the building of the railroad bed across the Keys in the early 1900s which united small islands with fill), an islet at the end of the Middle Keys group. The 1870 census noted it had 1 house and 13 residents.

G.S.

July 13, 1872. This day the Principal Keeper Mr. Peter Crocker, returned from Key West; he having left this on the 6th instant to bring up a new keeper as he said - he had tendered his resignation a month previous. On his arrival he handed me a letter from Superintendent's Office apprizing me of my being appointed pro-tem, he also said that boat now in sight has your two assistants. On the arrival of said boat Mr. Robert H. Saunders and J. Hiram Seymour both presented their appointments and entered on their respective duties. Mr. Crocker, and his assistant Charles Crane, left, after my having signed the necessary documents prescribed by rules of the establishment. About forty minutes before light up time I with the two assistants went up to the lantern room to instruct them in the usual routine of their duties. All went well till 10:20, when I came down to get a cup of coffee as I intended to remain in the tower all night. In less than 20 minutes after my leaving I was called loudly for by assistant Seymour who has the first watch. On my getting up there I found the light out, immediately substituted the rod lamp. In the interim I made an investigation but could discover no cause that could occasion the lamp to act unruly. I took off the smoked tube and lighted and adjusted a clean tube but as soon as I attempted to put full flame up she again went as she had done before. My God, I exclaimed, what am I to do, there has been a trick played on me with this lamp for she never did this before. I can't dismount and mount a service lamp tonight with you raw recruits, that is certain, so I put her out, relighted, put on a clean tube and contented myself by carrying a secondary degree of flame, by this time it was after 1:00.

July 15, 1872. This day proceeded to examine No. 7 lamp. Now this lamp had been in use since I have been at this house and am perfectly satisfied that when she was put aside she was in working order; I also discovered one of her plungers bottom up, one side upward and the covering cup turned the fore part behind, neither would she send forth a steady flow of oil until I took her to pieces and replaced her plungers and her crown piece to correspond with the distinguishing marks placed thereon by the lampist, afterward she worked admirably well.

On [the] 21st I took assistant Saunders into Hog Key settlement for him to get a passage to Key West and bring up his family, and was told by some of the settlers how Messrs. Crocker and Crane watched the light that night the 13th instant and described how she was acting with me which when I was told by the people of Hog Key fully convinced me that the whole affair was a deep laid scheme and that Crane had abstracted the pin in his morning watch, knowing he would be far from the building before she would be lighted again, as we saw the boat that was to bring up Mr. Crocker go in at the Key the night before.

A. A. Seymour, Keeper pro tem[32]

Note, we the undersigned having read over what Mr. Seymour has written, concerning the disarrangment of the works of the lamp at the place, very ready endorse the same believe the same to be a malicious act.

Robert H. Saunders Asst. Keeper
Hiram S. Seymour, Asst. Keeper

1875
George Parsons' Visit
to Carysfort Reef Light

George Shetwell (or Whetwell) Parsons was born August 26, 1850. He traveled from New York to Key West and then to Miami arriving on November 21, 1873 and was resident there until May 7, 1875. In Miami he helped tend the store of Henry Barnes, also serving as the store's bookkeeper. His handwritten diary is in the P. K Yonge Library of Florida History, University of Florida. My thanks to Dr. William M. Straight and Arva Parks McCabe, both Miami historians, who allowed the use of their transcription of the diary. The following has been excerpted from it and from a piece with it Parsons entitled "Three Days Imprisonment in a Lighthouse."

G.S.

Feb 2nd 1875. Everything being in readiness, we started on our long contemplated visit to Carysfort Reef Light in the little *Pearl*, an open boat...for the purpose of obtaining coral as well as to see the light house....Fine passage to Turkey Point, a famous place for birds & oysters, around which we went to the bird rookeries as we wanted some birds & eggs. Found plenty of the latter in the mangroves & shot several birds, cormorants - very good eating after being parboiled. While rounding the point, we were gliding smoothly along when suddenly there was a great commotion in the waters under our boat & some huge fish, shark or saw fish, lifted the craft, loaded as she was, nearly up & out of the water, rather startling us, especially the helmsman, who thought we were gone. The boat probably struck the fish as it was indulging in an afternoon nap. It was proposed to camp in the near neighborhood for the night & finally with the aid of a lighted torch, night having caught us, just the place of all others, was found, right on the point & once used by Indians we judged as the logs burned in their peculiar way were found. It was the most picturesque camping spot I ever saw & seemed fitted by nature especially for our accommodation....The next morning after our coffee & cormorant, we were off....

Feb. 6th...down Key Largo we went, a strong breeze behind us, bound for Stafford's place[33] & Upper Sound Point it still being too rough weather to think of running out to the light. Leland said it was some twenty miles & late in the AM we arrived thankful enough to be where there was water & a probability of something to eat. S. [Stafford] was absent when we came but appeared later having seen us a mile or so below where he was loading his schooner with buttonwood for Key West. Before he came though we had gone through his place pretty thoroughly finding nothing however but a few wild pawpaws & young cabbages in the way of food. Plenty of water. We had our greedy eyes on a few fine chickens, as were gone & we were hungry & as matters were approaching a crisis when the man's coming frustrated our plans. He came, I think, just about in time for our stomachs were getting away with our consciences & it was a question whether in half an hour, one of the fine looking hens would not have clucked her last. S. was very glad to see us, but had nothing to offer in the way of grub so it was arranged that he & I should try the fish & turtle tomorrow.

Sunday, February 7th 1875. It being a case of necessity, S. & I started off this AM & returned about sundown with two green turtles & a great quantity of crawfish (something like the Northern lobster) beside any number of snappers & grunts...We cooked & eat and eat & cooked & eat again until we began to feel rather scaly. A full stomach made a light heart & we felt pretty good tonight, it being the first time in some days we were permitted to partake of food & water unrestrictedly. We were Roman Catholic today, attending mass, a mass of the best fish every seen....

Feb. 8th, 1875. Well, at last I am come to the time, we all longed so for, a time when it would be advisable to run out to the Reef. This AM seemed to be our only chance & although wind & water were not such as we would have chosen with plenty of time on our hands, it was determined to make the attempt & accordingly we ran along Key Largo to Basin Hill the nearest land to the Light House, where we leapt off before the wind & in due course of time reached our objective point, Carysfort Reef & Light. When first heading for the light house it appeared in the distance to be a small, insignificant affair, but as we gradually neared it borne on the crest of tremendous waves its insignificance disappeared & gave place to wonder & astonishment & such a tower of strength & miracle of endurance. Approaching it on the northern side as directed, we anchored just within a line of breakers, with the keepers assistance ourselves & luggage were then transferred to the platform about twenty feet above the water & boat secured by two anchors & several cables. We were kindly received by the Cap & his two assistances & were made to feel perfectly at home in this strange place....

Presently we go up the iron stairs into the first room, a large one...Here we see the oil tanks one immense water tank holding two thousand galls. of water, much more of course than would be needed for these men...to supply any vessel that may be short of the article. Here is the place where the cooking & eating are done. Going up a half a dozen steps we are in the...hall...with three very pleasant rooms adjoining, all opening onto the balcony which extends in a circle around the outside. Here is the promenade where the spy glass is used & where we spent a great deal of our time gazing far out into the Gulf [Stream] & down into the waters below at the purple & indigo colored fish & other curiosities of the reef....

I understand the regulations require that all assistance should be given vessels in distress by the keeper & many is the craft Cap. Edmund Bell[34] during his five years stay has guided into a place of safety & grabbed off the rocks at low water. The reef for a considerable distance around may be seen & in the immediate vicinity of the light house on the southern side a person may walk about on the rocks & coral though not with dry feet. The tide rises & falls from two to two & a half feet becoming higher in Spring tides. There is a continuous roar from the breakers rolling in from the Gulf & spending their fury on the rocks in front of and below the light house & the wind which seems never to cease blowing, but keeps up a monotinous kind of music around here & there...[during a gale or hurricane]...the tower will shake as if keeping time with the wild melody without.

Then we were presented a treat. Cap B. brought out the *N. Y. Herald*, *Times* & their papers only four or five days old which he had received that very day from the S. S. *City of New York*, one of Alexanders Steamers, the Captain being so kind as to run in as near as possible & drop overboard to the keeper who was in his small boat, the package carefully done up so as not to be injured by accidently falling in the water. A pleasant day the head keeper often runs out in his little boat a hundred yards or so when he sees the right steamer coming & receives any number of papers, those on board well knowing what he wants. Running South the steamers skirt the edge of the stream as close as possible, going sometimes within two hundred yards or less of the light house & steaming North they keep well out into the Gulf or Straits as this part of the stream is called, to feel the full force of the current. We eagerly devoured the news feeling right near home for the time being.

A short while before sunset we followed the keeper up the winding stairs...we go up the few steps to the narrow platform between the lenses & outside windows, we are requested to be careful & not touch the glass, a precaution we are careful to observe, especially when the keepers themselves are required to don a loose blouse of some soft material to keep any buttons from contact with the glass. We now commence a study of a first order light; but before we are taken inside the lantern our attention is called to the reflection of the sun, sky & waves on the prisms & I never saw anything that could equal this beautiful picture of nature's own work, done on glass. Finer than the most delicate painting, reminding me of the finest tracing on ivory, this picture stood by itself & was worth the trip alone. The sun shining within the lenses, stamped out Henry LeSaules name & we much interested to see how the lamp is supplied continually with oil...the oil being forced into the lamp incessantly running over into the reservoir below. Four wicks constituted the lights & these took an immense chimney to cover them. The outside wick being four & one half inches in diameter circular in form. The best kind of land oil made for the purpose is used...

At precisely sunset, Cap B. & the first assistant with their lucerns (no matches allowed) enter the lanterns & ignite the wick in four different places; Cap. in the chimney, attach the smoke stack & set the oil feeder in motion; while the second assistant winds up the heavy, twenty pounds weight...now the light is lit & is shining a distance of 16 1/4 nautical miles, flash visible 18 1/2. The dome shaped lens is about ten feet high & consists of the upper & lower prisms, throwing the light down & up to the flame & thus concentrated it is magnified to the distance, maintained by the lens. It is like looking into one immense kaleidoscope to be under the lens & see the gorgeous colors and tints reflected by the prisms as the lens slowly revolve from left to right, once in eight minutes interval of flash thirty seconds, fifteen seconds light is seen & then it is eclipsed that length of time, an equal division being made by means of the brass framework into which the prisms & lenses are fitted...Now the Captain has to regulate the clock work, leveling the lenses & finally bringing the motion to the required rate, adding weights or taking off. Now he has time to talk & tells us about the birds flying past sometimes looking like great balls of fire & how he was once struck by lightning while near some of the machinery & many other things for the Cap is a great talker & a good one....The lenses & prisms cost $22,000 in addition to the house itself, which was put up in [the] North & then taken down in sections & shipped to these parts. As it is only at certain times that work can be performed out on the reef it is easy to see that the expense incurred in the construction of these light houses must be enormous....

Leaving the watch room we passed downstairs to the promenade & looked at the rays from the light above us stretching far out over the waters until they seem to be lost in them. They were very beautiful to see but here one can hardly turn around without seeing something to attract his attention & admiration at the same time & it seems almost useless to attempt to describe what one must see for himself to appreciate fully. Treats like this happen once in a lifetime perhaps & I consider myself as highly fortunate in being allowed the pleasure I have experienced. The first watch from sunset to ten o'clock now commenced. The second is from ten til two & the third & last from two til sunrise. Each keeper following in regular routine.

Now...for the first time we were to experience...sleeping in a light house. The wind & waves were fierce indeed. Old Boreas concluded it was time to visit us with another Norther & inside it seemed as though a violent gale was in progress, causing us much uneasiness for the safety of the boat; the Cap too, was alarmed as frequently during the night he visited her.

The next morning, we went out the long staircase before sunrise to see the "Gleam doused" in sailor parlance...The big lamp was extinguished like any ordinary one, the cover placed over the lens & curtains hung to the windows, not so much to keep off the dust as to protect the lantern inside the lens from being burned, the lens acting & being in fact nothing more than immense Sun or burning glasses. When the sun is very hot the heat is almost intolerable in this part of the castle in the air; although the place is well supplied with ventilators all open during the day but closed to the windward through the night so that no current of air shall affect the flame. Watching the sun rise at this elevation with nothing but a wide waste of waters all around as far as the eye could reach was a new sensation to me that would probably have given rise to some poetical effusion in one more sentimental than myself, the occasion being certainly worthy of the effort....

Rather cool this AM, the thermometer at 58 degrees, the lowest point reached this winter here. After dinner...the tide had fallen sufficiently to admit of our trying for some coral...the cool N.E. wind blowing & sending the breakers well to those places where we were to work & there was danger to be apprehended from sharks & morays in the many holes, still we were not going away without making the attempt as coral was what we came for & this was our only chance....

Very little progress was made in some time towards obtaining the coral & it did seem at one time as though we were not to have any. But we were more persistent than the waves & secured a few good specimens by one of us sitting on the other & holding him under water while the under fellow pried with the crowbar & gathered some salt water into his system as well as some nice looking coral into his hands....Were in the water not far from an hour & when we hauled ourselves up by the rope & stood on the platform we presented a spectacle that was truly heartrending. Shivering & teeth chattering while blood was running from numerous cuts & wounds & we were well nigh exhausted by our hard struggle with the waves & desperate exertion to detach the coral...

Wind fresh all day with heavy sea so no chance of leaving. Additional cables were made fast to the sloop today & another anchor added to the two already doing duty & it will certainly not be the captain's fault as he himself said if she is lost for nothing more can be done. The same entertainment in store for us again tonight & there was certainly no diminution of interest on our part, rather an added curiosity about several things that were thoroughly explained.

Feby 10, 1875. Imagination can do most anything in its line, but it is not very hard work to imagine ones self at sea...in such a position as we were, as but in reality minus the sea sickness, motion of the ship & attendant discomforts connected with a sea voyage. Here we were stationary, it is true but almost seemed by me almost in motion as vessel after vessel passed to North & South...That day as we watched the great ships tossed about in the Gulf Stream by the huge waves which seemed to be enjoying a holiday so boistrous & merry they appeared & angry at times as they seized great ocean steamers & flung them from them as pleased their fancy; sometimes sending them skyward & anon dashing them to earth again with a vengeance that would cover the good ships with foam of their wrath.

The third day & still we were by no means unwilling as every day brought its own interest....The captain himself said that although he has been there more than five years yet he's continually discovering something interesting & fascinating in nature & time never hung heavy on his hands, although his duties are light.

The waters about there seem to be alive with fish of all kind & description, color & hue & it would be very natural indeed to suppose that the table was well supplied, but strange as it may seem, the keepers never touch them owing to the fact of their being poisoned. Cap. Bell thought they eat some poisonous substance growing on the reef or else they are sick fish coming there for some medicinal property known only to them, a grand hospital...The Gulf Stream is clearly defined that it seems as though a pencil mark on paper could not divide the white from the black more distinctly than that does the adjacent waters from itself & has such an unusual steady flow it reminds me of the "Wandering Jew" going on forever....

Tonight we were treated to a lecture by the philosophical Cap. as we promenaded the leeward side of the balcony, on the applicability of the small affairs of life to the larger ones, were told the story about the lion & the little mouse, the little ass & the big man, etc. Our Aesop the Second waxing warmer as he proceeded, seeing how we appreciated all of his remarks.

Feby. 16th 1875....After breakfast we packed...including a remembrance in the way of a piece of coral given each of us by Cap. Bell & very shortly were prepared to leave...Our stay had been a remarkably pleasant one to all hands, even the nights we enjoyed, able to sleep without the smothering accompaniment of a cheese cloth mosquito bar. Although they have mosquitoes out there at times, as testified by the mosquito bar in the different rooms....

Well, now I have everything in my journal I can think of relating to the light house except the maintaining of two flag staffs, insignificant of themselves but of great importance when the one facing the Gulf is used for signalling vessels & the other to notify wreckers of a vessel ashore. Our light house system is said to be the most complete in the world & surely in all of its details & provisions it reflects great credit upon the National government. The Florida reef is well guarded now but two additional lights are to be erected & then it will hardly seem possible for a vessel to be "picked up" either by accident or design. Everything & body were now ready & nothing but the "So Long" was to be said. There was quite a sea & our boat secured as she was could not be handled from the distance, so I took a line and dove off of the iron steps into the waves coming up near to the boat into which I scrambled & we soon had her nearby, not very close however as the sea was very heavy & bounced her around pretty well making Ewan sick... F. declared it was suicide to attempt going ashore but was overruled & after all the luggage & coral were lowered into the boat, F. & D. got in the best way they could & in a few moments we were off, our cockle shell flying to heaven & then dropped into the trough of the sea, shot around by tremendous waves & making frantic leaps until finally smoother water was found & we sped along before the wind... Made "Old Rhoades [Key]" & then came into Caesar's Creek to hunt for treasure upon information received at the light house. Searched some there, of course without success & then ran up the outside of Elliott's Key aways, stopped for pepper coral & sea plumes. Camped about dark in a pretty good place.

Feb. 12, 1875....Slowly made our way home just about in time to keep a party from coming after us as it had been reported that we were all lost.

1925
Clement Brooks:
The Sea Left Carysfort Reef

Clement Brooks was in 1925 the second assistant lighthouse keeper at Carysfort Reef Light. The following is excerpted from his 1980 letter to Love Dean, in the historical collection Dean donated to the Monroe County Public Library at Islamorada.

G.S.

One particular time I was taking my nap when the captain walking the bridge stopped at my window, said, 'Get up and see the ocean going dry.' He was not mistaken - the tidal breakers were not breaking over the reef anymore. It was calm, parts of the reef showed out of the water. I lost no time for questioning [the phenomenon] - slipped into my swimming trunks, took one of our buckets which the captain let down on a rope. I was going hunting for sea shells. I saw some purple sea plumes half out of the water. I tried to break one off the coral where it was attached. I had to go back to the lighthouse and asked Captain Pierce to drop me down a saw or hatchet. I took my bucket back with small size sea fans, some yellow and others purple. I also put in some bunches of coral all grown together. My pail was heavy. He pulled it up. I dove down into a small pool, opened my eyes part way, got my saw set and went to work.

I had it about [sawed] through and I began to worry...I could feel the force of small waves dashing my feet and legs back and forth. I could tell the ocean was filling up again. Soon would be at top level of 30 ft., 15 ft. low tide. [What I was sawing] snapped off near the end - was I happy!! Up I came headed toward home plate. The captain had elbows over the rail shouting loudly, 'Hurry up Brooksie Boy, you're going to get wet!' He could see 8 ft. waves rolling in. I breast stroke part of the way when my feet weren't touching anything, [got to] the ladder, tied the saw and pretty sea plumes to the rope. That dry look happened twice while I served at Carysfort. You bet I did not go out quite so far [the second time] but did gather a few more curios.

1927
Love Dean's Interview with Charles M. Brookfield, Visitor to Carysfort Reef Light

This interview with Miami resident Charles M. Brookfield was conducted and taped by Dean in the 1980s and donated by her to the Monroe County Public Library at Islamorada. The tape was transcribed by Jim Clupper, Head Librarian, who brought it to my attention. In it Brookfield expands on his visits to Carysfort Reef Light.

G.S.

Dean: I have the privilege of talking with Charles Brookfield and I want to find out from him about some of his first trips on his boat *Manatee*, which you built yourself, or had built, as a fishing boat, basically. How large was the *Manatee*, Mr. Brookfield?

Brookfield: Twenty-six feet.

Dean: And she drew how much?

Brookfield: Twenty-six inches.

Dean: A perfect boat for the Keys. And when did you first go out to Carysfort Light? Do you remember?

Brookfield: I think it was 1927. I first visited the lighthouse, the first lighthouse I had ever visited, and the keepers were there. Very kindly people, especially Captain Pierce. He took me all through the light and explained how the lens operated and how it was fueled with the kerosene that had been vaporized and reheated in the coils first, and then there was a big...gas mantle like the old gas lights, and this was larger than they ever used at home when I was a child. Also, it had to be burned off just like the lanterns that campers use - kerosene.

Dean: So they were still using kerosene in 1927?

Brookfield: They were using it then and right up I think until the light became automated, and of course now it's all lighted with electricity.

Dean: There were three or four keepers on the light?

Brookfield: There were three keepers but only two at a time on the light. One was always ashore.

Dean: Do you remember their names?

Brookfield: Well, in the case of Capt. Pierce, I was there for just a brief visit and he had an assistant there with him whose name I don't recall. I couldn't help remembering Capt. Pierce because he was a very outstanding sort of a man.

Dean: Do you know what he did before he was a light keeper?

Brookfield: No, I don't.

Dean: How long had he been a light keeper?

Brookfield: I only knew him for the few hours that I was there on the light. But I was so impressed with their isolation. There were no radios in those days or anything like that and they were stuck out there. Stay for a couple of months with no refrigeration. They had to bring their own food of course with them because they paid for their own food.

Dean: Did they have ice or anything like that?

Brookfield: No, no, nothing like that. Maybe they brought some with them when they first came, but that would be gone in a day or two. But I was amazed with the cleanliness of the dwelling and the light. There was not a speck of dust anywhere. I doubt if they just dusted all the time. I think it was just because it was nearly seven miles from the nearest land that there wasn't any dust.

Dean: But they were very neat besides being very clean?

Brookfield: Oh, yes, all of the brass measuring utensils and everything that they used in connection with the light and its service was shiny and bright; it was a nice place to visit - Carysfort Light.

Dean: And then you started going out to the light every now and then?

Brookfield: Well, next time I went, it probably was about six months or so later. And, I didn't know, the personnel of the light had changed. I thought I was bringing some goodies out to Capt. Pierce. I brought some fresh meat and some fresh milk, newspapers...

Dean: You brought these things down from your own place on Elliot Key?

Brookfield: No, at that time I didn't have the lodge. I didn't build the lodge until about ten years later, but I wanted to show my appreciation. It was a different crew aboard the light. I didn't even stop to find out what their names were because the sea was running pretty high and you would have to run up to the light in a little open space about as big as the average bedroom that had been blasted out by the engineers while they were building the light so they could get their piledrivers and equipment up on the reef itself. That was where a small boat could come in, and that was where the iron ladder from the lower platform of the light came down to the water, so you could get up to the light. I just passed all these things up to the men on the light but I didn't see Capt. Pierce. I didn't know the names of the men then, but the next time that I came out to the light, which wasn't too long after, a nice, beautiful calm day, and I could hear them calling, "Here comes Santa Claus." They didn't recognize me, but they had made a mental note of the boat which brought these things there. I was welcomed, of course, aboard the light that time. Met Capt. Jenks and his first assistant, Harry Baldwin. They were aboard the light at that time.

Dean: And you stayed overnight at the lighthouse?

Brookfield: Yes I did, that night and that was a most interesting night [See "The Ghost of Carysfort Light" in Part 3]....But they were such kindly people. There were two keepers, of course they were middle aged men. By that time they had a telephone. It was amazing. Due to the efforts of our Congresswoman, Ruth Bryan Owen, who may have visited the lights herself way out there on the reef. There was a cable that ran all the way on the bottom. You could see it from the lower platform or up higher on the light you could see this cable....

Dean: How often did you go out there?

Brookfield: Probably went once or perhaps twice a year.

Dean: You did some fishing?

Brookfield: We used to fish for fun off the lower platform. There were big schools of snappers, and chubs, all underneath the platform of the light. All kinds of tropical fish like trunkfish and colorful tangs, and parrotfish, swimming in and out of the coral caves below, and all down the reef.

Dean: Did the lighthouse keepers tell you anything about their lives? I mean, it was isolated. Did they get many visitors?

Brookfield: No, very, very few visitors. When people came there they were usually so occupied with fishing that they had not time to spend to go on the light. They were catching fish like mad, which you could do there, mostly barracuda. When you hooked a small barracuda, say one that weighed maybe fifteen or twenty pounds, you very seldom ever boated it, because a much larger one came around and cut it in two, and all you would have would be the head and that's all. Really marvelous fishing. And even in the parlor, as they called this hole that had been blasted out back when they were building the light, and where you could come in with the boat, even in there, were some great big black groupers, huge ones that would come out once in a while into the parlor. The keepers had tried to catch those big black groupers, but there was no chance, fishing from the lower platform with a hand line. Because the fish would make for its hole in the coral and get themselves wedged in there.

My brother, Tom Taylor, was one of the most interesting people I have ever known. He was one of those "unique personalities" that one rarely gets to meet in a lifetime and I'm so glad and proud that he was my brother.

Tom always had a creative imagination and Tom's imagination enabled him to become a time traveler! As a young boy, Tom's imagination led him to the romance of tall-masted sailing ships, and to the silver rails of the "Iron Horse" - the American railroad. At an early age, Tom was a gifted artist and draftsman - he did beautiful pen and ink drawings of trains and sailing ships. He even carved scrimshaw, and he carved incredibly detailed sailing ships out of wood.

Tom's imagination allowed him to time travel to the era of the Revolutionary War, which he studied as a boy. And as an adult, Tom became an historical re-enactor. He was a member of the Coldstream Guard, among other groups, during the American Bicentennial, and he also performed in England and France.

Everywhere Tom went - whether it was a living history show at an elementary school (where the highlight always was Tom firing his musket) or a tour of an historical site, Tom entertained and excited folks with history!

When Tom was in the sixth grade he was already preparing himself for his future roles in movies such as "Glory" with Matthew Broderick - by becoming a producer/actor in a series of Civil War movies that Tom shot with an 8mm camera. Tom started the Civil War Centennial Club, and we made some hilarious movies - but they were historically accurate!

For example, Tom would zoom the camera in on a map of the Battle of Bull Run, then zoom the camera over to a supposedly dead soldier on the battlefield (covered in ketchup), who would start to laugh, roll over, and walk away! Hedge apples were our cannon balls and a cement wall in the field across from our house was Fort Sumter! His Ohio history teacher, Mrs. Glenn, was so impressed with Tom's ingenuity and his knowledge of the Civil War that she gave him a rare set of authentic military books from the Civil War.

Tom's imagination also led him to become an explorer. Tom - who loved God and country - loved to explore God's wonderous natural environments. He loved to sail the seas and to SCUBA dive under them. And he was also a rugged mountain climber. He tried the most challenging peaks in the eastern U.S. and he hiked the Appalachian Trail.

In his youth, Tom spent many summers in Maine, at Camp Kawanhee near Mt. Blue State Park. That's where Tom learned to love sailing and the outdoors. Also, our father was a minister to children who ran a large church camp in southern Ohio, so Tom grew up in a family that loved nature.

Tom's sense of adventure led him to live in Quito, Ecuador and in Mexico City before he was 21. He also lived in a tent for three years on Andros Island, Bahamas, running a field study program for marine biology students. Tom took students SCUBA diving in one of the most fascinating underwater areas of the world, and one of his students for a night dive was Jacques Cousteau!

Tom was a hard worker, and he turned his considerable mental and physical energies towards preserving history and the natural environment. Tom became an Historic Interpretive Specialist as a park ranger for the National Park Service, working at the De Soto National Memorial Park in Bradenton, Florida, the Castillo in St. Augustine, Florida, and Guilford Courthouse National Military Park in Greensboro, North Carolina where Tom rode and took care of Buck, the park horse.

Tom earned a Master's degree in Public History and Museum Administration from the University of North Carolina. He returned to Florida to become the Director of the Halifax Historical Society in Daytona Beach. He spent seven years as the research historian for the Ponce de Leon Lighthouse Association. He made the video that you see on the lighthouse grounds and developed many interesting exhibits there. In 1997, he was awarded the Lifetime Achievement Award from the Volusia Anthropological Society.

Tom was one of the founders and presidents of the Florida Lighthouse Association as well as the Florida Keys Reef Lights Foundation, and many other organizations we didn't even know about.

The body of his life's work is overwhelming to us - he did so much! Tom was a prolific researcher and writer; he has published books and produced historical documentaries that have been broadcast on the A & E and the History Channels. His last book, *Monhegan Island and Its Lighthouse* was written about one of his boyhood favorite lighthouses. He always told me that he would grow up to be a hermit on Monhegan Island.

We were hoping that when Tom moved down here to the Keys he would slow down a little - have more time to sail his *Ibis*. But everyone knows that it's not easy to make a living here, for the common man.

And that's what Tom was - he was the most Uncommon, common man. He had the kind of genius that revels in the pure excitement of the work itself - and Tom was then able to excite others. I will miss the amazing, interesting, good-hearted man who was my brother, Tom Taylor.

Saying Goodbye

I had breakfast with Tom in Marathon two days before he died of congestive heart failure. Everytime in the past five months we talked he told me (and others) of ill health, but all of us - including Tom - had no idea he was literally dying at the time. Four months before he died he couldn't even climb one flight of stairs - a man who once climbed to the top of lighthouses.

To try to assuage grief I tried to consider that he lived life on his own terms, had lived a life fuller than twenty other people put together, and did not know he was going to die, at a home he loved, that summer day in the Florida Keys.

In his papers Tom's mother found this poem, apparently selected when he himself lost someone close to him:

This is the place where we must sever
You go thousands of miles once, my friend, forever

Like the parting clouds we drift apart
But the sunset lingers like the feelings of my heart

- Li Bai
8th Century Poet

Beneath that was written, "the true feelings also of your fellow traveler/adventurer, Tom Taylor."

At his memorial service in Marathon his many friends from all over Florida boated out to Sombrero Key, the site of a lighthouse built in 1858. It was a beautiful day, and there were some ten boats anchored near the base of the lighthouse, where fish congregate because of the structure.

Children in the water were screeching in delight when tickled by the fish, which were gathering for the cheese whiz the kids were putting out to attract them. It was a perfect Tom Taylor scene, of joy and life, sailboats, the ocean, and a lighthouse. Flowers were dropped into the water from our boat, to drift away with the tide, as another of Tom's friends said a spontaneous prayer. It ended in the words I will never forget because they are so true:

"And we are thankful for the time that we knew you."

Gail Swanson
Fellow Traveler/Adventurer

Editors' Notes

[1] David L.Cipra wrote that the *Aurora Borealis* stayed at a dock in Pensacola, Florida until the summer of 1825 when she was ordered to Norfolk, Virginia and designated a relief lightship. In 1837 a request was made to Congress to repair her decaying hull. (Neil Hurley)

[2] In a letter dated November 7, 1831 from William Whitehead, Key West Collector of Customs identified one of the dead sailors as Hans Sodenberg or Hans Hansen. (Neil Hurley)

[3] In a letter of March 8, 1827, Key West Collector of Customs Pinkney reported to Steven Pleasonton that the "Alarm bell belonging to the vessel was broken by some contrivance of the man in question. I regret this very much as the bell was an excellent one and very costly." (Neil Hurley)

[4] In a letter dated May 15, 1834, Henry D. Hunter, captain of the U.S. Revenue Cutter *Taney*, described the Caryfort Reef lightship: "She is 81 feet in length, 20 feet 2 inches in breadth of beam and 12 feet, 4 inches depth of hold." The letter goes on to describe the ship as having a crew of a captain, one mate and six men. (Neil Hurley)

[5] A letter dated October 3, 1835 from William Whitehead, the Key West Collector of Customs to Steven Pleasonton describes the damage to the ship from the storm. Many of the glasses and fixtures to the lanterns were destroyed making it impossible to show a light from the ship for several nights. The anchor windlass was badly damaged as was the deck cabin. Both of the ships boats were lost with one being found sunk. The letter concluded with "The gale was more severe than any one that can be recollected." (Neil Hurley)

[6] Arron Carter, a black man who was probably a slave, was killed in the attack on Cape Florida Lighthouse. The temporary keeper, John W. B. Thompson survived the attack despite being shot six times. (Neil Hurley)

[7] The 1837 book *Territory of Florida* by John L. Williams states that Whalton had a small plantation planted with fruit trees. It was located about a half mile up Tavernier Creek. (Neil Hurley)

[8] A letter dated June 27, 1837 from William Whitehead to Steven Pleasonton also relayed news of the attack. The letter says that the attack was made by a group of 6 Indians who hid behind some casks near the shore. (Neil Hurley)

[9] The contract for the Northwest Passage light vessel called for a ship 68 feet long at the keel (78 feet long on the decks), 24 feet wide and 9 feet deep in the hold. The masts were to be 50 feet tall, double masts four feet apart fore and aft. (Neil Hurley)

[10] A letter dated December 17, 1840 from A. Gordon, the Key West Collector of Customs to Steven Pleasonton states that "The repairs of the Light Ship at the North West Bar are so far forward that the new Lantern is lighted, tho it has not yet been raised to the head of the masts. As it now stands a little above the deck, it is vastly more powerful than the old lanterns..." (Neil Hurley)

[11] A letter dated June 28, 1841 from L.W. Smith to President John Tyler reports that Captain Jeremiah Cottrell, late keeper of the lightship, was tarred and feathered and rode about the streets of Key West by a mob. Cottrell was suspected of poisoning his daughter. He was ordered to leave the city with his family which he did so immediately. (Neil Hurley)

[12] In a letter dated September 15, 1841 from A. Gordon to Steven Pleasonton it was reported that the ship's anchor windlass and bitts were carried away by the storm. (Neil Hurley)

[13] While contemporary reports talk about the construction works at Coffin's Patch being damaged in the hurricane of August 1856, it seems likely that the work on the lighthouse began at Sombrero Key. A letter from A.D. Bache to the lighthouse board on June 30, 1854 states that "A light on Sombrero key would guide vessels clear of the Patches, and could be made a more permanent work." Later confusion probably resulted from the earlier plans and appropriations made for a lighthouse at Coffin's Patches. (Neil Hurley)

[14] Diagonal astragals aren't necessarily thinner. They do ensure that the panes of glass are more parallel to the light source (allowing the light to pass through better with less bending) and they also ensure fewer "dim" spots since vertical astragals would block the light from some directions. (Neil Hurley)

[15] Charles M. Johnson, Jr. was the son of a notorious wrecker of Key West - who lived part time in New York City - Charles M. Johnson, Sr. (b. circa 1773, d. 1828) and Hannah Johnson (d. 1839). His brother and sisters were John W. Johnson, Amelia Johnson Sawyer, Emeline Johnson (b. May 1, 1812, m. Francis Watlington, the captain of the lightship *Florida*, and who lived in Key West's Oldest House) and Louisa Johnson (m. Nicholas Herder) (Gail Swanson)

[16] The letterbook is in National Archives, Record Group 45, Naval Records Collection of the Office of Naval Records and Library, Letter Books of Officers of the U. S. Navy at Sea, Vol. 13 PC-30, E.395 Subseries E-8 (3 of 8). (Gail Swanson)

[17] The Case of Ten New York Marine Insurance Companies vs. Charles M. Johnson (Binder of materials primarily from the National Archives, Northeast Region, researched, compiled, and transcribed by Gail Swanson for Nancy O. Jameson; copies placed in the Monroe County Public Libraries at Key West and Islamorada and in the P. K. Yonge Library of Florida History, University of Florida, Gainesville.) (Gail Swanson)

[18] Possibly John Disney - part owner with William Bunce of the wrecker *Thorn* and the *Greyhound*, and of the firm of "Bunce and Disney." There was another Disney in Key West at the time, however, one Thomas Disney. (Gail Swanson)

[19] Temple Pent, a Cape Florida pilot. (Gail Swanson)

[20] The log is on microfilm at P. K. Yonge Library of Florida History, University of Florida, reel 97G. Pam and John Viele provided me with their transcription of same from which this is copied. (Gail Swanson)

[21] London. Public Record Office, file reference ADM 1/3322. (Gail Swanson)

[22] *Savannah Georgian*, January 21, 1828. (Gail Swanson)

[23] Letter quoted in *Royal Gazette* (Bahamas), January 5, 1828. (Gail Swanson)

[24] *Niles Register* (Baltimore), Feb. 2, 1828. (Gail Swanson)

[25] *Royal Gazette* (Bahamas), Jan. 5, 1828. (Gail Swanson)

[26] Report of P. C. Fuller, Committee of Claims, February 4, 1836 in House of Representatives Report No. 4, 25th Congress, 2d Session, 1837. (Gail Swanson)

[27] London. Public Record Office, file reference FO 5/236. (Gail Swanson)

[28] London. Public Record Office, file reference FO 5/236. The report to the collector of the port mentioned was probably lost in a Treasury Department fire in Washington in the 1830s. (Gail Swanson)

[29]Sally Whalton personal collection of Whalton family papers. (Gail Swanson)

[30]This date was interpreted as 1830 by the library archivists - the handwritting being difficult to determine. Also, John Whalton had crossed the "l" in his name as well as the "t" making his name read "Whatton." (Gail Swanson)

[31]The letter was printed in Guido C. Levetto, *The Mist of Yesterday* (1994). (Gail Swanson)

[32]Adolphus Seymour was Assistant Keeper April 2, 1872 to June 30, 1872, then Keeper to November 1, 1873 when he was removed. He had formerly served at Sand Key and Northwest Passage lights. See Neil E. Hurley, *Keepers of Florida Lighthouses, 1820 - 1939,* third edition. (Gail Swanson)

[33]Per historian Jerry Wilkinson a Dennis Stafford, age 27, seaman, born in Ireland and owner of real property valued at $500 was listed in the 1870 census of the Keys. (Gail Swanson)

[34]Edward Bell was Assistant Keeper August 10, 1869 to October 28, 1869 when he was promoted Keeper, to January 17, 1881, when he was removed. He was born in England in 1831 and had formerly served at Key West and Sand Key lights. Neil E. Hurley, *Keepers of Florida Lighthouses 1820 - 1939*, third edition (1995). Historian Jerry Wilkinson has found that Edward Bell was the first land owner on Key Largo. He purchased six tracks of land from the state on March 3, 1876, and another three on October 1, 1880, all on north Key Largo and probably visible from the lighthouse. (Gail Swanson)

Index

Made in the USA
Monee, IL
07 July 2026